TRUE
POLICE
STORIES

About the Author

Ingrid P. Dean, detective sergeant, retired, worked with the Michigan State Police from August 1989 to April 2011 in a variety of capacities, including patrol work, polygraph, forensic art, investigation, and teaching.

Det. Sgt. Dean graduated summa cum laude from Wayne State University, Detroit, Michigan, with a BA in art. She obtained her master's degree in Transpersonal Studies from Atlantic University, Virginia Beach, VA.

Det. Sgt. Dean's research entails the collection of true, exceptional police experiences viewed as transpersonal—a school of psychology that studies the transcendent and spiritual dimensions of humanity. It is an academic discipline, not a religious or spiritual movement.

Det. Sgt. Dean is a licensed polygraph examiner for the State of Michigan, a basic scuba diver (PADI), and private pilot.

Do you have a police story of your own?

Please visit her website at www.spiritofthebadge.com and submit your story today!

TRUE POLICE STORIES

OF THE
STRANGE & UNEXPLAINED

Detective Sergeant Ingrid P. Dean

Llewellyn Publications
Woodbury, Minnesota

FIRST EDITION
Fourth Printing, 2018

Cover art © Fuse/PunchStock
Cover design by Adrienne Zimiga
Editing by Sharon Leah

Llewellyn Publications is a registered trademark of Llewellyn Worldwide Ltd.

Library of Congress Cataloging-in-Publication Data
Dean, Ingrid P.
  True police stories of the strange & unexplained / Ingrid P. Dean. --
1st ed.
      p. cm.
  ISBN 978-0-7387-2644-1
1. Parapsychology and crime--United States. 2. Parapsychology in
criminal investigation--United States. 3. Police psychology--United
States. I. Title.
  BF1045.C7D43 2011
  130.973--dc23
                            2011036077

Llewellyn Publications
A Division of Llewellyn Worldwide Ltd.
2143 Wooddale Drive-
Woodbury, MN 55125-2989
www.llewellyn.com

Printed in the United States of America

Contents

Foreword

I have been an intuitive all my life, but the majority of my working career has been spent in the fields of law and corrections. After earning a bachelor's degree in both psychology and sociology, I worked for fourteen years as a felony probation officer. This job required a great deal of contact with police and other corrections workers. During that time, I also did post-graduate work in criminal justice studies and ultimately earned a Doctorate in Law. I was in the private practice of law for many years prior to leaving it to pursue my writing and speaking career full time.

Because of my unique mix of intuitive ability and legal and criminal justice training and expertise, I was asked to train police officers to use their own intuitive abilities in their work. For many years, I was honored to share this training with a number of different police departments. Police officers are, while highly intuitive, also very guarded about sharing personal stories and experiences. As a matter of fact, I can think of no other group of people who are less likely to openly discuss anything that might be labeled "paranormal" or "metaphysical."

On the whole, police and corrections officers have more than their share of intuitive ability. As a matter of fact, it is a necessary tool that an officer needs to be safe and successful. Among themselves, many officers call this skill their "blue sense." It is the ability to just know things without quite understanding why. It is the sense they have in their "guts," or how they "smell" out danger. However, the officers I worked with and trained were very reluctant to claim this ability. When I would ask for examples of intuitive instances in their careers, I was usually answered by silence. More often, an individual would privately come up to me after a training session or during a break to share a story of intuitive insight.

That is why I was so impressed when I read Ingrid Dean's book, *True Police Stories of the Strange & Unexplained*. Because she, herself, is a detective sergeant, she was able to elicit stories from her fellow officers about amazing occurrences of psychic ability, Divine intervention, ghostly apparitions, and much more. These stories are even more impressive when you consider who is telling them.

Of the thousands of people I have trained to master their intuition, police officers are, in many ways, the most difficult subjects. This is not because they do not have ability. This is because they are very selective about who they trust and careful to only state "facts." Police officers are trained to write highly factual reports. They are not encouraged to speculate or give opinions, and they certainly are not allowed to include flights of fancy or unsubstantiated information.

As you read these stories, you will see how their training is now used in their accounts of metaphysical and intuitive events. Because I know police officers so well, I chuckled a bit at the details included in their stories. Their training and experience shows as they recount names, times, and other information as factually as they recite the most amazing of unexplainable phenomena.

This collection of stories is fascinating and intriguing, and also deeply touching. The police heart shines through the pages in the kindness and concern shown by these hard working and honest officers. I only wish that this book had been available for me to use as a manual when I was doing my trainings. Despite my education, degrees, and correctional experience, I was never completely accepted as "one of them." This is perhaps the most impressive thing about *True Police Stories of the Strange & Unexplained*. Only another police officer would ever have been trusted enough to be given these accounts. Thanks to the courage of the officers who shared these stories, we have ample proof that there are many things beyond what we can see with our physical eyes and experience with our five senses.

Police officers deal in life and death situations. They are, perhaps, the most likely people to see many unusual and bizarre happenings. For them to step forward and share them with us is a gift. I am very grateful to Ingrid Dean for collecting these accounts and I hope she continues to receive many more. These stories are the best proof I have seen of intuitive knowledge and paranormal happenings.

—Kathryn Harwig
Author and Intuitive Master

Introduction

A human being is part of the whole, called by us "Universe,"
a part limited in time and space. He experiences his thoughts
and feelings as something separate from the rest—a kind of
optical delusion of his consciousness. This delusion is a kind
of prison for us, restricting us to our personal decisions and
to affection for a few persons nearest us. Our task must be
to free ourselves from this prison by widening our circle of
compassion to embrace all living creatures and the whole of
nature in its beauty.

—ALBERT EINSTEIN

When I first entered into police work, I thought the law enforcement profession was all about service, caring, and making a difference in world. On one level, it certainly is. After over twenty years in the field, however, I've learned that police work is much more. It is really an avenue to see oneself through other people. It is an opportunity to address one's deeply held convictions about life and death and the make up of the world.

Not anyone can be a police officer. It takes an extremely courageous, patient, and relatively balanced person to do this job successfully, productively, and honestly. It takes stamina and resilience to make it all the way to retirement. Most importantly, good officers must be willing to see and understand themselves inside—the good, the bad, the beautiful, and the ugly—in order to really do this job effectively. In my years of service, I have learned to see people more as reflections of myself, in varying degrees. Whether fellow police officers agree with me or not, I believe we chose our jobs to try and heal ourselves.

Police work covers a much broader spectrum than most people realize, concerning human nature and the perils of life and death. Television and the media hardly touch what we really do. As I approached my eighteenth year of police service, I suddenly realized just how narrow-minded and ill-educated people are about police officers—even some administrators and experts in law enforcement, who seemingly forget or have never experienced what it is like to work the streets. I also realized that some of my greatest pleasures and pains came from my own brothers and sisters within law enforcement. I had a realization that police work isn't just about serving the public, although that is certainly very important. The journey also includes mirroring each other inside police work.

Hence, this book—a compilation of exceptional human experiences that share and explore how police officers, the public, and life and death are interconnected. It is an attempt to share the full spectrum of extraordinary, strange, and often unexplainable situations police officers experience in their job. I want people to see that there is a human being inside the uniform and behind the badge. It is my hope that fellow police officers can connect with the reader and the public on a more spiritual and emotional level.

This is not a Harry Potter book. It is not a book of scholarly writing. These are *real, true stories.* The police officers who wrote them possess varying degrees of writing skills and talent. The collection is made possible by the collective contributions of many active and retired police officers and fellow workers in the field. They speak from their souls.

I collected these stories from officers during the past four years. I chose this assortment of experiences so every reader might find at least one account that touches, heals, or rattles their soul in a positive, educational way. You may not agree or concur with every story, because the stories fall within such a large range of perspectives—from the ordinary to the extraordinary. All I ask is that you be gentle and thoughtful with your opinions. These officers are speaking from their perceptions. Regardless of religion or beliefs, every story seems to suggest we are multidimensional beings. They also imply that our outer and inner worlds are probably much bigger than we think they are.

Lastly, I know of no other books where police officers have openly shared about unexplainable phenomena or their epiphanies, so I pray you have great fun and enjoyment reading this book. Strange things *do* happen! Police officers are very reliable, credible people who seldom lie. They learn to laugh and cry in their jobs—they just don't always show it.

Thank you to all my fellow police associates and friends who entrusted me with their remarkable stories. You are so daring and brave! I am so grateful to have you as my family.

—Ingrid P. Dean

one

Angels & Divine Intervention

Shared observances and interactions with angels and Universal/God thought are valuable. They expand our grasp of possibility and multidimensionality. While death may remain a physical reality from a scientific point of view, great questions about the real meaning of "terminal" and "eternal" are raised by these recorded experiences. The occurrences certainly lessen the sting and fear of death. They demonstrate the interconnectedness we've been learning about throughout the ages.

An Angel's Shield

In 1992, I worked the 12th precinct (now the Western District) of the City of Detroit in a marked, uniformed patrol unit. My regular partner and I had been separated by a shift supervisor who didn't like either one of us. I was paired with a desk officer who had little street experience. As we went out on the road, I hoped it was going to be an average day.

As it became dark, we found ourselves driving north on Wyoming Road near Santa Clara. There was a red light at the intersection and all traffic was stopped. The car in front of us was occupied by three guys and had license plate BNL661 (I'll never forget that number). The car stopped momentarily and then drove through the light. My first thought was that the light was stuck, but then it turned green.

The occupants of nearby cars looked at my partner and me as if to say, "You're the police. Do something about it."

We activated our lights and attempted to pull the car over. The occupants began to argue. We could see them yelling at each other. They weren't going fast—just cruising—but they weren't stopping the car either. I advised our dispatcher of the situation and the direction we were traveling. Then the car turned down a side street and parked.

Instinct told me to stay further behind than I normally would on a traffic stop. As I started to exit the patrol car, the person in the front passenger seat leaned out of the door window and fired at me with an Intra-tech 9mm Uzi-style weapon.

Everything happened so fast. He fired at least three shots before I realized we were under fire. I quickly re-entered the police car to get to the radio to call for help. I shouted, "Officer in trouble! Twelve-11 under fire!" As I reached for my weapon, I could see bullets tearing through the metal hood of the patrol car on an angle toward the driver's door—my side. I knew I'd be hit if I exited.

Then the gunman fired a shot directly into the windshield of the patrol car at face level. I should have been killed. It should have hit me directly in the mouth. However, the bullet flew up, deflecting off the windshield. I knew the windshield wouldn't take another hit without being penetrated. I had no choice but to get out of the car to fire because my shots were not effective from a seated position.

As I started to leave the car, everything went into slow motion. A golden light filled the car and I heard a calm male voice say, "Don't worry. You're going to come out of this fine. You won't be hurt." I believed the voice. It felt as if a shield had been raised up in front of me. I knew that I wouldn't be hurt!

I exited the police car while the gunman was still shooting. I aimed and fired my weapon, causing the driver to floor the gas pedal and speed away. I emptied my magazine as the gunman and his accomplices fled.

I was not harmed at all. I looked around and saw my partner's hat in the street; the passenger door was wide open. The first thing I thought was that my partner was hit. I searched around the patrol car and advised dispatch that I couldn't find my partner. Moments later, additional police cars arrived, one with my partner in the backseat. It turned out my partner ran from the gunmen after the first shot.

Physically, I had been left alone—but spiritually, I had the best backup in the world. I am alive today because of divine intervention.

—*Stephen C. Sokol, officer, retired*
Detroit Police Department

Wake Up!

It was close to midnight. I was very tired after working the afternoon shift, and I was driving home alone toward Adrian, Michigan. I was still in uniform, driving about sixty-five mph along a highway with farming fields on both sides when I fell asleep at the wheel of my small pick-up truck.

Just as my vehicle hit the gravel on the shoulder, I heard a loud voice shouting, "WAKE UP! WAKE UP!" I opened my eyes and realized I was headed straight for the north shoulder of the road.

My head was tilted forward, and I knew I had been sound asleep. Awake now, I looked toward the passenger seat and saw a man sitting there. He was staring me in the face, leaning toward me, and yelling at me to wake up. I could only see his outline because a bright glow seemed to come from within and around him. We were looking at each other eye-to-eye, but the brightness was so great that I could only see the contours of his face and body. I'll never forget his intent stare.

I immediately looked forward and realized I was approaching the top edge of the ditch. I didn't panic. I took my foot off the gas and steered back toward the roadway. Once I had the truck under control, I looked toward my passenger again, but no one was there. A dim light was still glowing, but it soon faded away.

It was not a dream. I saw a man, and I felt his presence in my truck. He was very bright, which gave me the impression he was an angel and not an ordinary ghost.

This is an experience I will never forget. If I had driven off the roadway at the speed I was going, chances are my truck would have flipped and death or serious injury would have been the consequence.

I truly believe a guardian angel saved my life that night.

—*Herman Brown, trooper*
Michigan State Police

The Helmet

As a United States Army military policeman assigned to the 9th Infantry Division in Vietnam, I had many duties, most of which my recruiter failed to tell me about. One of these duties was to provide security to the combat engineers as they performed mine sweeps of the major highways. For safety reasons, this was done very early in the morning before traffic began moving.

Our platoon was located at Fire Support Base Moore just outside the Cai Lay District in the Mekong Delta, about sixty miles south of Saigon. It was always hot. The average daily temperature there is between 105 and 110 degrees Fahrenheit. We rarely wore a helmet or flak jacket, which helped keep us from getting too hot.

One day, we received an order from our provost marshal, Lt. Col. Phillip Ash, stating that it was mandatory to wear the helmet and flak jacket at all times when outside of our camp. The very next morning I was assigned to the mine-sweep detail.

The Viet Cong had been very busy the night before putting out mines on the road. When the combat engineers find the mines, they safely detonate them and fill in the holes and repair the road. They had found a very large mine and detonated it, which left a large crater. All traffic had to be stopped while they filled the hole and repaired it.

As I stood in the middle of Highway 4, holding back the traffic, a bus kept edging forward toward me. It brushed up against my leg. I moved forward just a little, and so did the bus. I walked around to the door and entered the bus. I told the driver he could not move any further until the hole was filled and the road repaired. Then I left.

As I walked toward my jeep to tell my sergeant what had occurred, I heard a loud explosion. I turned around to see this same bus flying up in the air. The enemy had placed a plastic command-detonated mine in the road. Because the mine was plastic and contained no metal, the mine sweepers had not detected it. The explosion killed more than half of the people on the bus and seriously injured the rest.

As I stood there in shock, I realized that Sgt. Murphy, whom I had just spoken to, was near the bus when it blew up. I ran to him and observed him standing there with shrapnel holes in his flak jacket and his pants torn, but he was not hurt.

Then, all of a sudden, we started to receive rifle fire from the enemy. I hit the ground, crawled back to my jeep, got the microphone to the radio, and called for artillery support.

After all the action was over, we grouped together to make plans to treat and evacuate the wounded. At that time, one of my brother MPs looked at me and asked about the hole in my helmet. I had no idea what he was referring to. I took off my helmet and was surprised to see a hole in it. Luckily, the bullet that pierced the helmet itself had stopped in the helmet liner.

If it had gone all the way through, the bullet would have hit me just above my left eyebrow.

I thought back to the order our lieutenant colonel had put out the day before that required all MPs to wear their helmet and flak jacket. If he had not done this, Sgt. Murphy and I would not have survived the attack. As I reflected on this, I also realized that less than two minutes before that mine exploded, I was standing directly on top of it. To this day, I do not understand why I survived and the people on that bus died.

Nothing in this world will ever convince me that this was something other than Divine intervention. I took a magic marker and wrote the words "God is my Partner" over that bullet hole, and I never let that helmet leave my possession during the rest of my tour in that country.

In 2007, I was planning a reunion for my Vietnam Unit and I contacted Lt. Colonel Ash. When I told him that story and I thanked him, his words to me were: "Well, son, it's a good thing you followed orders!"

—*John Patterson, sergeant, retired*
9th Military Police Company, United States Army

The Bone Lady

We are called to a drowning. A snowmobile with two riders has gone through the ice. We dive in and find the snowmobile, but no bodies. The sheriff contacts Sandra Anderson, a woman who is famous for finding bones and bodies in water. This is my first contact with the Bone Lady.

Sandra brings her dog. She says her dog can smell the gasses emitted by dead bodies, even in water. After a couple of hours she announces, "The dog is indicating the bodies are not out there."

"How can you tell?" I ask.

She says, "Well, I can tell by the way the dog acts." A week later one of the bodies shows up—only about 150 feet from where we were searching. This is my first red flag that something is wrong with the Bone Lady.

My next contact with her is in regard to a woman, Cherita Thomas, who has been missing since 1980. We believe Cherita is a homicide victim. McGregor and Dave Marthaler (FBI) take Sandra in the woods to search for Cherita's remains. The first time they search the woods, nothing is found. They take Sandra to the same area a second time, and they start finding bones. I photograph the bones and e-mail the photos to a forensic anthropologist. He says they are animal bones. I recall Sandra telling me that her dog would *never* hit on animal bones. Another red flag is raised.

I start to get bad vibes about the Bone Lady. She always wants to *return* to a site ... she never finds bones the first time, only on the second or third visit, and in areas that have already been thoroughly checked.

By this time, the crime team has discussed other missing people with Sandra. We have provided all kinds of information to her, and she continues to return to the same areas where she's already been. Miraculously, we start to find human bones. We even bring in the FBI Recovery Team on one of the searches.

We are on a suspected location and the dog is marking areas. To indicate the location of a bone, the dog puts its nose to the ground and then lies down. Sandra sticks a flag in the ground wherever the dog does this. We start searching the flagged areas. Several of us are down on our knees in one area when the Bone Lady says, "The dog is indicating there is a bone over there."

"Where? Where is he indicating?" I ask.

She says, "Over there. Right where he's at..."

I look again and say, "We've already looked over there. There's nothing there. Where do you mean?"

She says, "Right there. The dog is sitting on it."

"How can you tell the dog is sitting on a bone?"

"I can just tell. He's sitting on it," she says. "Reach underneath him and grab the bone!"

I thought, *Yeah, right. I'm going to reach under the dog and find a bone ... this is a joke!*

She sees the look on my face and says, "I'm serious!" She moves the dog up, and low and behold, the dog is sitting on a bone!

The anthropologist on the scene determines it is a finger bone. "Yeah, it's definitely human," he says. Then he sticks it up to his nose and says, "Smell this."

I look at him incredulously as I think, *Right, the dog's ass was just on this bone and now you want me to smell it ...*

He says, "Seriously, tell me what it smells like."

I put it under my nose and sniff. "Smells like chlorine bleach."

"I was thinking more like ammonia, but yeah, bleach or ammonia," he says.

"Why would this bone smell like ammonia or bleach after all these years?" I ask.

We discuss the possibilities. The best reason we can surmise is that the murderer poured chlorine bleach or ammonia on the body when it was decomposing to get rid of the smell. We search further and find more human bones.

Meanwhile, we are still searching for Cherita Thomas. John Lucy and Jenny Patchin from the crime lab have joined us, and the Bone Lady is here, too. On one of our previous searches, Sandra was told about two hunters in a white Ford Bronco who have been missing since 1969. Well, she confused Oscoda County, where that case happened, with Oscoda, Michigan, which is far away in Iosco County. One of the finger bones she discovered on this search was wrapped in camouflage material—as if there was still flesh on it. It seemed to me that Sandra was finding evidence for every crime we told her about in this one area, like it was a mass dumping ground for bodies in Iosco County.

Anyway, everybody on the team believes the bones Sandra finds are real. They are excited about the discoveries, but I am getting strong feelings the whole time that something just isn't right.

Sandra marked areas in a nearby stream a year ago. As we are walking along, the dog hits on something in the stream. Sandra sticks flags in the water and says, "Let's come back to this. Let's go search another area first, then we'll come back here."

"Whatever," I say, although I think it is odd.

We follow Sandra and the dog to some other areas. She wants to look at what she calls coyote dens. She thinks coyotes drag body bones to their dens. Muskrats live in the banks of the stream, and she thinks the muskrat holes are a coyote den.

Someone finds a broken bone underneath a stump and everybody gets excited. "Hey, man, look we found an arm bone!" The anthropologist confirms it is an arm bone.

Sandra then announces, "Well, I'm going to go back down to the creek." She meant where she had earlier planted the flags in the water.

Realize that John, Jenny, McGregor, and myself have already sifted this area with screens—right down to the hard bottom of the stream. We removed all the muck and did not find anything. I decide to accompany Sandra to the stream.

She kneels down in the water and says, "It's gotta be right here, gotta be right here. The dog says it's by my foot, dog says it's by my foot …" I see her hand go to the back of her leg. "It's gotta be by my foot."

Jokingly, I grab her foot in the water and say, "Hey! I got a WHOLE foot!"

"No, no, seriously," she says, "it's gotta be right down here by my foot." I take my hand off her foot, and sure enough, there is a bone right by her foot. The bone looks really old and brown. "Oh, you're so good!" she says. "You're always finding bones! Now, let's check this other area where the dog says there's something." She kneels down in the water and starts searching.

As I watch Sandra in the water, I realize she always wears leg warmers with her boots untied halfway down. There is usually a lot of bulk on top of boots.

Sandra says, "It's gotta be right down by my foot, the dog is saying something's here."

So I reach in and, sure enough, there's another bone. "Boy, these things look like they're one hundred years old!" I say.

"Maybe you found an Indian burial ground or something," she suggests.

I'm thinking, *No, this is too coincidental ... two times in the stream ... in areas that have already been sifted ... just her and me ... no ... something's wrong ... it's all just too coincidental.* Of course, I don't say anything. After all, she is famous. She's known worldwide for her work. I don't feel like I know enough yet to question what she is doing, but I do have a *sick* feeling in my head and heart.

All of us are at the "coyote den"—the Bone Lady, Dave, Allen, and me. Sandra starts poking a stick in an overturned tree and says, "The dog indicates something is underneath there, something is underneath here. It's gotta be here ... gotta be right here."

So, I get down on my hands and knees and start crawling into this hole.

"Geez," I joke, "I'm going to get my ass bit by some muskrat!"

"Oh no," she says, "the dog says something is there."

Crawling in the hole is like crawling under a desk. It's a smooth sandy area where the water washed up from the creek. It's all clean sand. There is nothing there. I come out of there laughing. "Hey, there's nothing here."

"Hmm," she says. "Dog is tired, better go. We'll come back tomorrow."

Dave and Allen go back up the bank. I start to follow, then turn around. There's Sandra on her hands and knees, and she says, "My boot came untied ... hey, I see a bone!"

"What do you mean you see a bone?" I say in disbelief. Of course, everybody turns around and comes back.

She points. "It's right there! I can't reach it though!"

The hole is about an arm's length away. I get on my knees and there, where before there was nothing, is a bone sticking out of the sand. I *know* that bone was not there ten minutes ago. Now, I really am sick, because I know Sandra is planting bones at this crime scene.

I don't know who to talk to about this. Sandra gives me a hug and says, "You're so good ... you find all these bones!" I think to myself, *Yeah because you just put them there!*

We call it a night and leave. All the other guys are saying, "This is great! We're finding human bones! How exciting!"

I go home thinking, *How am I going to say anything when they're all so excited? She's a famous lady, and I don't have proof— but I know I'm right.*

The next morning, before we return to the scene, Jenny and John come to me. Jenny says, "Do you think we missed anything when we originally searched that stump and found only beaver chips and stuff like that?"

"Not unless it was something so small you couldn't see it," I answered.

Jenny shook her head. "No, I'm asking you if you think we missed anything like this?" She pulls out a piece of fibrous carpet material about two inches by one inch in size. "Do you think we missed this?"

"NO WAY! No way," I say.

"Sandra went back to the stump and said we missed this," Jennie says.

"Let me tell you what I think is going on." I tell them all my suspicions and end by saying, "I think she's got to be carrying bones in the back of her pant leg, in her bunched up leg warmers. I think Sandra is physically planting the stuff."

We decide we're not letting Sandra out of our sight. One of us will stay with her at all times—no matter what—all day long.

Unfortunately, Sandra manages to walk off with Al and Dave. They are headed to the other coyote dens with the dog. *Damn, now she's out wandering around and none of us are with her!* Sandra "finds" a piece of bone that allegedly has feces on it, which the anthropologist from Michigan State University is able to match with one of the other bones. Sandra wants to return to the stream, because the dog has alerted her.

Jenny says, "I'm going with you." The two of them go off together. McGregor is at the creek, too. Sandy kneels down in the water and starts feeling around. Jenny is watching. She sees Sandy's hand go behind her leg and reach at the back of her boot. Sandy says, "Oh, I got the bone right here ..." But Jenny grabs Sandy's hand before it can touch the bottom and says, "Yeah, because you just put it there." The two women get into a tug-of-war over the bone!

Sandra tries to throw it back in the water. Imagine that! A bone that she just found—and she wants to throw it in the water! Well, McGregor is trying to figure out what's going on. He grabs the bone, and that's when Jenny and I tell him, "She's planting the bones."

I was relieved that with the help of divine intervention, Jenny and I connected that morning. Otherwise, the charade would have lasted much longer. Eventually, it was found that the bones were from Louisiana State University's medical department. A captain in the fire department, who trained cadaver dogs, was allowed to have the bones, and he was supplying them to Sandy. Some of those bones ended up on our scene.

The FBI charged Sandra with ten counts; she pled to five. Some people have appealed their cases based on her finding some of the evidence that convicted them. Fortunately, the evidence she found was just one small piece to the puzzle in each case. She would simply "find" the piece that investigators thought they still needed to tie up their cases.

Sandra has served her time and was recently released from federal prison.

—*Mark A. David, chief of police*
Oscoda Township Police Department, Oscoda, Michigan

This Time, I Was the Victim

It was early in the 2003 holiday season when my wife and I were invited to a holiday fund-raiser at a posh restaurant in Detroit's Indian Village area. The purpose was to raise money for less fortunate inner-city kids, so they could be supplied with shoes for the upcoming winter.

I did my homework on the event. The mayor and some federal judges were also invited, so I trusted that their security details would have things well in hand. Thus, I did not fear for my wife's and my safety or that of the other guests, including a police lieutenant from my department and his wife.

It should be noted that a police officer is **always** on duty. When we take the oath of office, most agencies require us to carry our gun and badge twenty-four hours a day. We are rarely allowed to let our guard down. If we do, we are often criticized for it. In this case, I did not have my gun with me. I consider that divine intervention in and of itself.

The entertainment, food, and drinks were fantastic. It was a very nice evening, even though the mayor never showed nor did any of the federal judges or other celebrities as promised.

Things were winding down for the evening. The valet girl found me and gave me the keys to my vehicle, saying she was going off duty and would no longer be responsible for my truck.

Then, she ran out the door.

I went to the door to look for my truck, saw it, and was returning to the restaurant when two gunmen broke in! They rushed me with a gun pointed directly at my face, grabbed me by the necktie, and forced me into the dining room. One of them fired a shot next to my head and announced the hold-up. I went to the ground. A second shot was fired and fragmented when it hit a $40,000 grand piano. A fragment of the slug struck a lady.

I was not armed, as I believed the mayor's security detail would be present. It's a good thing I wasn't, because I am positive that if my weapon had been seen I would have become another Detroit homicide statistic.

I believed I was going to be shot in the head as I lay face down on the floor. I threw my cash on the floor, as the gunman demanded everybody's wallets. My wallet had a badge and police ID in it, and I knew that if my identity was revealed, I most assuredly would be shot.

For some unknown reason, I envisioned a crime scene photo with me lying face down on the floor with my brains spilling out of my skull. I was not about to allow that to happen. My wife was only a few feet away, hiding underneath a table. She appeared to be okay.

I began to pray and felt the presence of a guardian angel. The fear left me and I was able to focus on the criminals' actions so that I might become the best witness and see them led off to prison in handcuffs.

I threw my wallet under a table and it landed face open with the badge in full sight. I flipped it closed. How they never saw this had to be the work of an angel.

I was kicked in the groin as the number two gunman gathered up the cash and wallets. They went to a second dining room and I heard screaming and another gunshot. Then all was silent. I immediately called 911 to report the armed robbery with shots fired. I was still on the phone when the first patrol officer arrived and started to calm everyone and check for injuries. Before I knew it, there were uniformed officers all over.

Suspects were being picked up in the neighborhood and brought back to the scene, but I couldn't identify any of them.

My wife and I were thankful to go home alive that night with only relatively minor injuries. About a week later, we were sitting in our kitchen having our Saturday morning coffee, watching the local Detroit news program when I saw a story about a major arrest having been made by the Violent Crimes Task Force, a team comprised of FBI agents, Michigan State Police troopers, Detroit police officers, and some suburban Detroit police officers. The number one gunman's mug shot was displayed and I immediately recognized him as the one responsible for the armed robbery where we were victims.

All weekend I telephoned the investigator assigned to our case, with no reply. Monday morning, I was able to contact a member of the Task Force and tell him our story. The bad guy, who had been arrested along with four others, was responsible for murder, armed robberies, and carjacking. A fifth suspect, a juvenile, had fled to Alabama, and the FBI was after him. Their specialty was robbing patrons at fund-raisers.

Weeks later, I was able to pick him out in a line-up at the Wayne County Jail. Although I never saw the case go to trial, as the number one suspect had already been convicted of first degree murder and sentenced to life without parole, I believe it was the intervention of an angel that saved my life that night. Divine intervention led me to watch the local news channel and see the scumbag's mug shot.

—Steve Standfest, lieutenant, retired
Beverly Hills Police Department, Beverly Hills, Michigan

Oh Ye of Little Faith

I was on patrol when a 911 went out about a person hit by a car. A ten-year-old girl had been hit by a pick-up truck traveling sixty-five mph. When I arrived on the scene, she looked like an adult, because her body was so swollen. Both arms and legs were broken and turned in the wrong direction. I had to adjust her head three different times to keep her breathing.

She and her sister had been running down the side of the road to meet their father, who was on his tractor plowing a nearby field. The victim ran ahead of her sister and was turning around in the road to run back to her sister, when she was hit. Unfortunately, her sister saw it happen. The father was now at the scene.

We had the girl air-lifted to Detroit Children's Hospital. Since it was the end of my shift, I didn't phone the hospital for an update until the next day. I was certain the case was a fatal accident. The hospital spokesperson would not give me the list of injuries, even though I was the investigating officer. I explained I already knew she had two broken arms and legs. "I'm sorry. You don't understand. It is not that we *won't* give you this information, we just *can't*. All I can tell you is that she has spent eighteen hours in brain surgery and it looks like she's going to live."

I said, "So what does that mean?"

The nurse said, "She's probably going to be a vegetable, but it looks like she is going to live."

I thought to myself, *Oh God! Why didn't you just take this ten year-old girl, instead of letting her live the rest of her life as a vegetable?* It upset me. I reflected on this for awhile, then let go of the matter entirely—at least that's what I thought.

About six months later I was giving a career day talk at Brown City Elementary School when a girl came up to me. "You don't remember me, do you?" she said.

I said, "No."

She said, "You were there when my sister got hit by the truck." My heart sunk deep into my chest. I realized I hadn't really let go of the issue.

I didn't know what to say, so I asked, "How is she?"

"She's doing great!" the girl answered. "Sometimes she forgets what happened a long time ago, and sometimes her left arm goes numb, but she is almost ready to come back to school! You should stop by our house because my parents would really like to thank you."

When I heard this, I thought, *Oh, ye of little faith*. My faith in God and the power of Divine intervention was restored. I was reminded that I became a trooper to save lives and that I do make a difference in the world.

—*Mary M. Groeneveld, trooper*
Michigan State Police, Stephenson, Michigan

An Angel's Warning

When I was young, my mom said she had a guardian angel to watch over us, especially whenever we traveled or did something risky, like race motorcycles. She said she always sent along her angel to take care of us.

Both of my parents died in 1987; my dad from a long battle with cancer, and my mom of a broken heart (they died within twelve hours of each other). Since then, I have always known that my mom's angel watches over us, and I have called upon her many times to protect my own kids.

In 1997, another trooper and I from the Detroit Post volunteered to transfer to Benton Harbor. I figured Benton Harbor would be a lot like Detroit, plus it would be a break from the regular stuff at the Detroit Post.

Benton Harbor *was* a lot like Detroit, just on a smaller scale. One common practice when we came to a red light while patrolling was that if traffic was clear, we treated the light like a stop sign: stop, look both ways, and then drive through. The philosophy was to get the job done and not waste time sitting at a red light.

On one particular night, I was driving and we had been "stop signing" red lights all night. About three in the morning, my partner and I approached a green light at a blind intersection in downtown Benton Harbor. The tall buildings on all corners prevented me from seeing any possible oncoming cars. I said to my partner, "We've been going through red lights all night, I think I'll stop for this green light and balance the scale." I had no sooner stopped at the light when a car came screaming around the corner and drove at a high rate of speed through the red light!

If I had not stopped at the green light, we would have been broadsided. My partner and I looked at each other in amazement. Both of our jaws were dropped as we stared at each other in awe. We both knew we had been divinely protected. I knew my mom's angel had saved me once again. (Of course, we chased down the car and took appropriate action.)

—*Robert Marble, trooper*
Michigan State Police, deceased

Breaking the Rules

While I was on patrol, an oncoming vehicle sped by me at almost 100 mph. I had a feeling that something was wrong and that this wasn't just a speeder gone wild. I made a U-turn and promptly stopped the vehicle.

A man jumped out of the driver's seat and frantically ran toward me. He cried desperately, "My son has been stung by a bee and he's *dying*! Can you help us, please? He's in back of my car. He can't breathe!" I saw the boy's head resting on his mother's lap; he was gasping for air.

The couple did not realize that the hospital they were heading for had recently closed its doors. Even though I was a fairly new trooper and still conditioned to following protocol, I decided to use my God-given power of discretion. There wasn't any time to wait. I piled both parents and their son in the backseat of my patrol car and headed for the nearest hospital.

I drove faster than I'd ever driven before—even faster than in recruit school. The boy was suffocating. It was obvious his throat was swelled up, and he appeared to be losing consciousness.

Boisterous from adrenaline, I said to the boy, "Hey, look! All the cars are pulling over for you! Wow, they see our lights and sirens! How do you like being in a patrol car and riding so fast? We'll be at the hospital in no time, sweetheart."

I was probably more excited than his parents. I don't know how I kept my voice from cracking. I kept urging the parents to keep him awake. I was so scared for the boy.

It was summertime and with all of the tourists in town, traffic was bumper-to-bumper. As I wove safely between the vehicles, I knew divine intervention was at hand. We didn't encounter any backups or delays.

Other thoughts rushed through my head, though, such as *Will I be reprimanded or fired for this?* I knew calling an ambulance would have taken too long, but I was breaking departmental rules. I considered pending lawsuits. I finally shut out those thoughts and silently affirmed, *I don't care if I'm written up. They can fire me, if they want. The boy is hurt. I know I'm doing the right thing. I'm following the voices of my angels.*

We arrived at the hospital in less than ten minutes, and the boy was rushed to emergency care. The parents thanked me repeatedly, and then I left. I returned to my daily business, though I wasn't looking forward to seeing my desk sergeant, because I was certain I would be confronted.

Later that day, when I returned to the post, I was surprised to learn that the boy's parents had stopped by to thank me again. Fellow troopers greeted me with smiles and the desk sergeant actually patted me on the back and said, "Kudos, kiddo. Good job, but get back to work." At the end of my shift I went home and thought the incident was forgotten.

When I turned on the eleven o'clock news, however, I saw the boy's attending physician talking with a news reporter. I thought to myself, *Wow, this made the news?* and I turned up the volume on the television. The doctor said, "... by far the worst case of anaphylactic shock I have ever treated. If that trooper hadn't brought the boy here so quickly, or had waited even five more minutes, this boy would not have survived." I chuckled and thought, *Well, that's cool. I hope my boss is watching this because everything I did was against the rules!* Then I shut off the TV and went to bed. I was content.

Divine guidance had directed me—and the boy was alive and well. Since I had broken departmental rules, I was disqualified for any life-saving award. But, one month later, I received a letter of appreciation from the governor himself! I laughed. The parents were so appreciative they had called the governor. I framed it and hung it on my wall.

To this day it reminds me that no badge or trophy can ever bring me the same joy as knowing those parents brought their boy home. Any material award would now be a total insult—to both me and my angels!

—Ingrid P. Dean, detective sergeant, retired
Michigan State Police, Traverse City, Michigan

Angel Voice

In the autumn of 1982, I was assigned to CID (Criminal Investigation Division) Special Investigations, working surveillance on Highway M-13 near Saginaw, Michigan. I was following an undercover officer (UC) and a dangerous suspect in a vehicle ahead of me. My job was to follow the car and keep the UC out of trouble—and to back him up if needed.

While driving southbound, I had just passed two trucks (a pickup and a semi) when a ten-year-old boy rode his bike out from his driveway directly in front of me. He was crossing the road and failed to look to see what traffic was headed in his direction.

I had two choices: hit the boy or swerve the car to the shoulder of the road. At the time, all I could think of was my own son, who was about the same age. I wasn't going to hit this kid, so I took the shoulder of the road.

Obviously, I was traveling above the speed limit to complete the pass and to keep the UC's vehicle in sight. I lost control of the surveillance car on the gravel shoulder. The car swerved radically back-and-forth and shot across the northbound lane of traffic (lucky for me, nobody was coming). The car hit a driveway culvert and then flew airborne over a four-foot ditch.

It is at this point that everything slows down in my mind. As the car is going through the air and I'm headed sideways toward a large tree in someone's front yard, I ask myself, "Am I going to be all right?"

A voice inside my head responds, "You'll be fine."

My car lands on the ground, the windows blow out and dust and dirt are everywhere. I am shaken, but fine.

As I pull myself out from the car, I wonder where the voice came from.

—Albert A. Boyce, detective sergeant, retired
Michigan State Police, Haslett, Michigan

The Power of Prayer

I was working in Cadillac, Michigan. Hansel Andrews, who was last known to have been with Robert Ostrander, was reported missing. After several visits to Robert's house and other locations, I could not locate either man.

About a week later, Hansel's truck was stopped by police in Las Vegas, Nevada. The occupants, who were known drug users, told police Misty Ostrander, Robert's wife, had given them the truck. This was my first clue that something was wrong and that Hansel was perhaps dead.

I considered it divine intervention that Hansel's truck was stopped by the police. My second intuitive thought was that this case was a drug deal gone bad. Although I didn't know if Hansel was alive or dead, I felt there was a criminal act involved in his disappearance. I pursued my follow-up investigation, assuming I would turn the matter over to some other jurisdiction located between Wexford County, Michigan, and Las Vegas, Nevada.

A few weeks after Hansel's car was confiscated, Robert and his brother's girlfriend, Analisa, were involved in a serious car accident. Robert suffered a broken leg and Analisa had significant head trauma. Upon Robert's release from the hospital, I met with his wife, Misty, who had come home from Las Vegas. Analisa was in the hospital several months before I was able to interview her. When Analisa realized I wanted information on Hansel, she refused to talk with me.

An informant, whom I will call John (to protect his identity), was arrested on an unrelated charge by my partner, Detective Sergeant Greg Webster. Special Agent Rob Birdsong of the FBI and I interviewed John because he said he had information about a homicide. I sensed it was about Hansel. I heard a voice pleading in my mind, "Please listen. John has something to say."

Michael Ostrander, Robert's brother, had told John that Analisa and Robert had been in the car accident when they were on their on their way to put gasoline on a grave site in the woods so that animals would not dig up a body buried there. John said the body was Hansel's.

John's sister allowed me to wire her vehicle and agreed to initiate a conversation with Analisa. In a recorded conversation, Michael admitted to John that Hansel had been shot and killed in the woods. John said he drove him somewhere in order to get rid of the gun, and Analisa went with them. Analisa said Hansel's body was buried near the area where she and Robert got in the accident. She didn't sound at all bothered by the situation.

A drunk driving warrant had been issued to Robert Ostrander following the car accident. With the assistance of the prosecutor and the FBI, we decided to use the warrant to arrest Robert in Las Vegas in order to extradite him back to Michigan. Robert pled guilty to the drunk driving charge and was sentenced to one year in the county jail.

It is interesting to note that it took my assistants and me almost a year to develop this case and to prove that Robert killed Hansel.

While Robert was in jail, he made several telephone calls. Most convicted felons know that all telephone conversations are tape recorded, so they often talk in code. Robert spoke with his wife, Misty, several times. In one conversation, he said, "No B, no C." It wasn't hard for me to figure out "no body, no crime."

In another conversation, Misty said, "I talked to my attorney and he said there have been very few times they have been able to charge someone without a body—only once in a great while." Again, I knew she was talking about "no body, no crime."

During the winter, my partner, Creed, and I decided to go to the area where the car accident occurred to look for possible grave sites. Creed and I walked, or drove, or rode on snowmobiles over and over, looking for clues during the long winter season.

I often felt we were close to the body. Mentally, I could hear a voice talking to me. Creed and I drove down one trail, just looking and probing, but fell short of the actual grave site by about one hundred feet. Yes, we were that close to the grave, but didn't know it at the time!

After more talks with John, he finally admitted to driving Michael, Robert's brother, and Analisa to Manistee and to throwing a gun off the pier. John also adamantly claimed that Michael was at the scene of the shooting. John said that logs were placed on the grave site to hide it and that Hansel's cell phone was tossed inside the grave on top of him, along with a slew of credit cards. John repeated how Hansel had said, "Wow, what a cool camp site" as he was getting out of his truck, not knowing his dreadful destiny. John also pointed out the two-track where Michael said Hansel was killed and buried.

Over the next several months, Creed and I looked for a "really cool campsite" and any logs that might by lying around. While we searched, a grand jury interviewed witnesses under oath. Analisa testified in front of the grand jury, but she lied about her involvement in the matter. A warrant was issued for perjury and Analisa was eventually arrested in Utah. At this point, Analisa finally agreed to talk to the police.

FBI Special Agent Birdsong and I took Analisa out to the forest where we believed the grave site was, but she could not remember where the body was buried. All she remembered was that her feet got muddy. Twenty acres is a lot of land to comb for one small man-made grave. As I drove through the woods, I said several prayers, hoping for a miracle.

Once again, at the now familiar trail marker, I turned down the trail. Although I had no idea why, the marker seemed significant. This time I drove farther than we had before and suddenly, only fifty feet off the trail, I saw a small sandy area with logs on top of it! The logs seemed out of place, because there were no trees like them in the area. The logs just didn't fit.

Then I spotted a blue laundry detergent container lying nearby. *Maybe this jug was used to pour gas over the grave*, I thought.

I got out of my vehicle, moved the logs, and felt soft sand underneath my feet. I brushed away the leaves that covered the forest floor. At first I thought, *Maybe somebody either used this as a hunter's outhouse or moved the logs over*, but then I thought, *no, this could be a burial site.*

Later, I obtained a soil sampler from the health department and probed two different times into the ground. The probe went down about five feet, but didn't hit anything. There was nothing unusual about the soil samples I dug up.

I also used a shovel to dig a small hole. I brought a cadaver dog out to the site, but it didn't hit on anything. I even took Analisa to the location, and she didn't recognize anything. I contacted the Michigan State Police Crime Lab and requested an archeological dig anyway, just in case.

Without any good physical evidence, there was no hurry to do the archeological dig. In fact, I didn't hold much hope that Hansel's body would be found.

One day, some narcotics detectives and I were looking again for the grave site. When they stopped to eat lunch near the site I'd already probed, I went off to look at a nearby creek area, because Analisa had remembered having muddy feet. After I left, FBI Special Agent Birdsong pointed to the sandy area and told his guys it was the type of area they should be looking for—a place where the ground was disturbed and were there were signs of human presence, like the logs and laundry detergent container.

One of the deputy narcotic agents asked Birdsong if they could just dig? Birdsong knew it probably wasn't good police work, because the crime lab had already been contacted to dig, but he reluctantly agreed. The deputy took two swipes with a shovel. The first wipe—nothing. On the second swipe, however, out popped a cell phone! The deputy instantly recalled that a cell phone had been thrown in the grave with Hansel. They radioed to me, "You're never going to believe this, but we found the grave site! This is it! It's the spot you originally picked out! Hansel's here!"

I thought they were joking—coworkers kid a lot—but I was in no mood to be kidded. The deputy sputtered excitedly, "I'm NOT kidding! Come see for yourself! We just dug up a cell phone!"

I didn't believe him until I saw the cell phone. The chills and relief I felt were indescribable. We called the crime lab and they agreed to start an archeological dig immediately. As the scientists dug, one by one, the credit cards John had mentioned were retrieved. Eventually, about forty inches down, they hit on the sole of a tennis shoe—it was Hansel. His body had been found.

We obtained a warrant for Michael's arrest and located him in Flint, Michigan, where he was hiding out. We obtained a full confession from Michael. He was at the site when Hansel was killed and it was his brother, Robert, who shot Hansel point blank. Michael confirmed that the incident was a drug rip off, just as I had guessed from the beginning.

Based on Michael's confession, we got a warrant for Robert's arrest—this time for homicide. It was only two weeks before he was to be released on the drunken driving charge. What divine timing!

Walking into federal court was like entering God's chamber; it was completely different than the everyday district or circuit court. The judge looked like an archangel. When it was my turn to testify on the stand, one of the defense attorneys asked me, "Can you tell us how you located this grave? How did you find it in the first place?"

After some reflection, I finally answered, "Sir, I said an awful lot of 'Our Fathers' and 'Hail Marys'. That's how I found the grave. That's how I found Hansel." (This exact statement is in the actual court brief).

I didn't expound upon the mysteries of the matter. I knew it was God working through me. My answer was perfectly honest—although I did have to explain more to the court.

—Daniel O'Riley, detective lieutenant, retired
Wexford County Sheriff Department

two
Intuition

The majority of committed, dedicated, and devoted police officers—regardless of their public image—will do whatever it takes to assist and resolve a traumatic or threatening situation, to the point that they go beyond self. They will go beyond their five physical senses—even if it entails a near-death experience. Psychic ability, intuition, and gut-instinct are not unique gifts or paranormal capacities, but rather abilities and skills that anyone can develop with practice. Everyone can discover and develop his or her talents and inner wisdom by using intuition, logic, and common sense to make the best choices.

Trusting Your Instincts

As a young trooper, I started my career with the Michigan State Police at the Ypsilanti Post. After two years there, I asked for a transfer to the Upper Peninsula since my elderly parents and in-laws lived on the west end. I got the transfer and was assigned to the Stephenson Post.

One night my partner and I went to look for an individual for whom we had a warrant. The warrant was for furnishing intoxicants to minors. The wanted subject was known to be at his deer hunting camp, as he knew we were looking for him. We went to the camp, only to find it dark and no vehicle around. Apparently he was not there. We looked into the windows with flashlights. I could see fresh food on plates in the sink. After looking through several windows, only one more remained that had not been checked. At that point, I had a strong feeling that told me not to look in that window. My partner did not want to look in any more windows, either. We left without incident.

The following day, one of our officers arrested the subject. He told the trooper, "If that trooper had looked into the last window last night, I would have blown him away." He had been sitting in the dark with a loaded .30-06 waiting to shoot me.

After learning of his intentions, I knew why I had had such a strong feeling to not look in that last window. Apparently, my partner was also uncomfortable at the time, since he instructed me loudly not to investigate any further.

—*Reuben R. Johnson, lieutenant, retired*
Michigan State Police

The Skull in the River

As a forensic artist and road patrol trooper for the State Police, I have worked on many interesting cases. Little did I know that a cardboard box placed on my desk one sweltering August day would contain one of the most challenging and emotional cases of my career. A year earlier I had completed a facial reconstruction course at the FBI Academy in Quantico.

The box contained a human skull and was my second skeletal case. The first case I worked on remained unsolved, and the charred body of a black female was still at the morgue, waiting to be identified. This new case held little more promise. It had already sat on a property room shelf for nine years.

As I leafed through the police reports, I learned that the skull had been dredged out of the Clinton River, which runs through Mt. Clemens, Michigan, in 1992. A construction worker on a bulldozer thought he had found a gigantic mushroom. When he jumped off the bulldozer to kick it from its position in the soggy marsh, he was shocked to discover it was actually a human cranium. The rest of the body, including the lower jaw, was never recovered.

Although missing-person reports were carefully checked, the skull remained unidentified and was packed away in a property room at the sheriff's office. In the summer of 2003, the property room was cleaned out and the skull was sent to a Michigan State Police crime lab for possible DNA and comparison purposes. One of the senior members at the lab suggested it be sent to a forensic artist to do a reconstruction. Several weeks later, the skull was placed on my desk.

First, I took it to the Michigan State University Anthropology Lab, where I asked the anthropologist to examine it and give me a biological profile of the person I would be reconstructing. He told me it belonged to a Caucasian male, between the ages of eighteen and thirty. Since I wanted to do a three-dimensional reconstruction with clay, the missing mandible posed a huge problem. The lab was nice enough to let me borrow a specimen from a body that had been donated.

I fished through several boxes of bones in the lab labeled "Caucasian males" before finding one with a similar bite pattern. With my borrowed jawbone and several x-rays of the seven teeth that were left in the cranium, I took the skull back to my post to start work.

For the next eight months, I juggled the reconstruction in between normal working duties. As the face began to emerge, I began to get a feeling about what this man must have looked like.

For instance, I could see that his teeth had been extremely well cared for. He could afford a dentist and he took good care of himself. From this I assumed his socioeconomic place in life. I also surmised that he was good looking. Since the skull was dredged out of the river in 1992, I figured he must have been in the water for some time to become completely disarticulated and skeletal. Therefore, I guessed his hairstyle would be from the late 1980s or early 1990s. I decided to sculpt a longer, falling behind-the-ears hairstyle, in brown, since that is the dominant hair color of the Caucasian race. I also gave him brown eyes—both an intuitive and practical guess. I reminded myself that a reconstruction doesn't have to look *exactly* like the person—but there has to be something about it that triggers a sense of recognition in just one person who sees it and thinks, *Hmmm, that might be so-and-so.*

Finally, in April 2004, the reconstruction was ready to be released to the media. I held a press conference and was shocked to find that almost every media source in the metropolitan-Detroit area showed up to get the story. The following days were filled with newscasts, phone calls, and interviews.

About a week later, a district sergeant who worked as an accident re-constructionist in my district phoned me. He had seen a photo of my reconstruction in the *Detroit Free Press* and it reminded him of a young guy who had gone missing from the Algonac area when he was a road patrol officer there. He said the guy's name was Shawn Raymond.

Since this was my first real tip, I didn't have any particular feeling or hope that this was going to go anywhere. I went to the Clay Township Police Department and asked if I could see the Shawn Raymond case. The officers were all too familiar with the case. Shawn's file revealed that his mother had reported him missing after he was not seen for two days. Shawn was nineteen at the time and a recent graduate of Algonac High School. There were several photos of Shawn in the file, including one of his high school yearbook photos. I noticed he was an incredibly good looking guy, with feather-brown hair and a glowing smile that revealed very white teeth—just as I had imagined.

I didn't immediately see a resemblance between the clay sculpture and Shawn, though I did notice Shawn's dental charts. There was crucial information on these charts. The skull and Shawn had the same two bicuspids removed for orthodontic purposes. This was a clue I could not ignore. I immediately took the case back to my post and began calling to locate Shawn's dentist to get x-rays for comparison.

The first call led me to a dead end, literally. The dentist's wife sorrowfully informed me that her husband's practice had closed after his death and she had destroyed all the remaining records, including the x-rays. My stomach lurched. I thought, *is this the end of my investigation?*

I feverishly pressed the keys on my telephone to call Shawn's orthodontist. Amazingly, he was still practicing in the area, and he still had Shawn's file, which included panoramic x-rays of Shawn's teeth. I picked them up a day later. I was ready to put my anthropology degree to the test and compare the dental films. As I drove back to the post with the x-rays, I phoned my dad, who has thirty years experience as a trooper, detective, and forensic artist. Feeling very nervous, I said, "It's got to be him. There are so many coincidences!"

My dad urged me to be calm. "Now, settle down. This is only your first tip," he said.

Back at the post, I scotch-taped the bite-wing x-rays I had taken at MSU to my office window, and then, with hands shaking, taped the panoramic film from Shawn's orthodontist file underneath it. Undeniably, even to my little-trained eyes … it was a match! Now all I needed was the final okay from an ontologist (forensic dentist). I sought one out in the area and made an appointment to meet with him at his office the following day.

It seemed like morning would never come. I had several conversations with my dad, who continued to tell me, "Don't get your hopes up too high." But I was beyond help. In my mind, I knew it had to be Shawn. There was nothing that was going to convince me otherwise (except, maybe, this expert I was about to meet).

As I drove to his office, I tried to calm myself down. I had thoughts like: *What if it isn't him? What if I have to start all over again?* My stomach was in complete knots. A soft rain was falling as I approached the parking lot and turned in. I made one last call to dad and told him, "I'll phone you with the answer as soon as I'm out!"

When I met the dentist, I sized him up to be on his last year or two before retirement. He was elderly. He had me set the reconstruction on a stool and took his own panoramic films of the skull through the clay. I guess he didn't like the bite wings I brought with me as proof. When his x-rays were developed, he held up Shawn's films and the freshly taken films to the fluorescent lighting above him. He nonchalantly said, "Nope, that's not him."

I was dumbfounded. My heart sank. I fought off tears and began to tremble. Here I was, in my professionally tailored uniform, holding a human skull encased in twenty-five pounds of clay, and I was fighting to choke back tears. I mumbled to him, softly at first, "No, you're wrong..."

As my vision cleared and I regained my composure, I took a quick glance at the films he still held in his hands. Still fighting tears of disappointment, I stated clearly and louder, without reservation, "No, you're WRONG!" I snatched the films from his hand. He had been holding one of the films *back-ward*! I handed them back to him the correct way. He raised the films toward the lights again and—without hesitation—said, "Yup, that's him!"

On the trip from his room to my car, it seemed like I was running in slow motion. Once I was in my car, I called my dad. "Dad, it's him!" And, for the next half-hour, I sobbed.

At least my tears were of joy and not sorrow. I was so glad that Shawn's family would find out he was no longer missing, and that his remains had indeed been identified.

Note: Facial reconstruction requires both scientific and intuitive work to successfully identify someone. Features such as the nose, lips, style of hair, etc., are almost strictly intuitive guesses.

—Sarah Foster, detective trooper
forensic artist/facial reconstruction, Michigan State Police

A Special Spot

Worried parents reported that their sixteen-year-old son was missing. They thought he had run away, but they had no idea where. When I arrived at their home, something didn't feel right. I asked the parents more questions than usual. I asked if the boy got good grades in school and if he had any troubles he was dealing with. They said his grades had gone down recently and that he was on antidepressants.

When the parents mentioned antidepressants, I got a very clear thought: *This is not a runaway complaint.* I don't know why the word *antidepressant* triggered this thought, because usually it doesn't mean anything to me. I know that antidepressants are often very helpful to people, even children.

I looked in the boy's bedroom and saw two unopened packs of cigarettes by his bed. I thought, *What sixteen-year-old boy leaves two packs of cigarettes behind?* Most teenagers carry their cigarettes with them, especially if their parents allow them to smoke. This was the second hint that the incident was not what it appeared to be.

I didn't want to, but had to ask: "Do you have any weapons in the house?" The father said yes and that he had already looked. All of the cases were present. I asked if he had opened the cases, and he said no. I told him to go check. When he returned, he reported that a rifle, a Ruger .280, was missing. I suddenly knew their son was probably dead, but I didn't say anything. Not yet. It was the third clear thought that came through my mind.

I got the urge to take a look outside. Sure enough, I found footwear impressions in the snow that appeared to be the boy's—and they seemed to lead into the woods. The snow was patchy this time of year, so I called dispatch for canine assistance. While I waited for the dog and handler to arrive, I telephoned the boy's best friend. I asked if there were any special spots where the boy might have walked. I knew most teenagers have one. Because the snow was minimal, I knew that even with a dog, it might be difficult to track the boy unless I had an idea where to head. Sure enough, the boy had a special spot.

When the canine officer arrived, the dog picked up a scent. It was an overcast winter day. The canine handler and I followed the dog that had picked up the boy's scent. I was glad I had called the boy's best friend for directions so that I knew we were on the right track.

As we walked, I realized how breathtaking this area is. The near-pristine woodlands, hilly terrain, and sand dunes of Leelanau County, Michigan, are absolutely gorgeous. The smell of the pines was pungent and pure. I thought, *What a pity this young man has taken his own life when there is so much to love about this land and life*. I already knew we'd find him dead.

We continued to follow the boy's scent. The trees opened up into a small open area in the woods. We found him at his special place. He had shot his head off with the missing rifle. I was so thankful I had trusted my intuition and hadn't allowed the boy's parents to come with us. The scene was too gory for any parent ever to see. Although it was hard and their grief unbearable, the boy's parents were relieved I had found their son.

I thought about this case several times afterward. If I had treated this situation like a routine runaway complaint, the boy's body might never have been found. Corpses are often eaten by animals—sometimes without a trace left—especially in this area of Northern Michigan, which is known for its vultures, eagles, and coyotes.

I am sure many of my fellow comrades also rely on intuitive thoughts. Most of us seldom, if ever, talk about it, of course. Policemen are expected to rely on logic and "just the facts."

I think we should use intuition, logic, and common sense in order to make the best choices.

—*Duane Wright, deputy*
Leelanau Sheriff Department, Suttons Bay, Michigan

NCO with a Gun

After finishing one of my tours to Vietnam, which included some heavy involvement in the TET 68 Offensive, I was assigned to the 96th Security Police Squadron, 96th Bomb Wing (SAC) at Dyess Air Force Base in Abilene, Texas. I was involved in many police incidents during my eighteen months at this base, but the most dangerous incident occurred one evening when a TAC (Tactical Air Command) NCO (non-commissioned officer) was seen in the NCO Club flashing a pistol around and making threats. The NCO Club night manager called the law enforcement desk and reported the incident. I happened to be working the night shift.

We arrived at the TAC barracks, had the Charge of Quarters on duty show us the room, and then we had him unlock the door. Interestingly, the night before this looming confrontation, "Adam-12" was on television and showed a fictional incident with a guy and a gun, shooting up the neighborhood. This affair was almost exactly the same.

A fellow tech sergeant and I, along with several other patrol units, responded, but the NCO had left before we got there. We interviewed several of the folks that saw the weapon involved. All of them knew the NCO who was assigned to the TAC Wing on base. We traced him down to the barracks he was living in. Two other security police NCOs and I went over to bring him in for questioning.

The lights were already on. We went into his room and announced ourselves. The NCO was laying in his bed with his clothes still on and with a shoulder holster still on him. As we walked toward him, my two security police NCOs had their weapons drawn (.38 caliber pistols) at the "ready position" in case this guy tried to pull a gun out. We came up to his bed, and with one of us on each side of the bed, tried to wake him up by talking to him.

When he moved a little and his right arm started to go under his pillow, I grabbed and held his arm down with my right knee and hands. The NCO on the other side grabbed his left arm and held it down as well. The third NCO "covered him" with his pistol. We then gave him warnings not to do anything that may cause him to be hurt or killed.

I had one of the NCOs take the pillow away to see what this man was looking for. You guessed it! A .38 caliber pistol! My sixth sense about danger seemed to be working accurately. We picked him up and handcuffed him. Then, we searched him. We unloaded the ammunition and secured the pistol. He was read his rights and told why he was being taken into custody.

He was transported to the law enforcement desk, and his commander was called to come and get him. We didn't know at this time, but we had screwed up the pat-down search. When his commander came in, he acted as if we were the problem, not his NCO. The commander, a major, said that this NCO had just returned from an overseas deployment to Africa and was going out again within a couple days.

Now, to me, this made the incident excusable and I thought we should just drop everything on the poor TAC NCO. Then came the "curve" from the commander. The major asked us what we did with the ammunition (six rounds of .38 caliber bullets) that was left in the shoulder holster after he was searched. We made a big mistake. One round was not accounted for when we looked again. The commander wanted to know what we did with the round.

It is not unusual for situations like this to happen in police work when officers get accused of something they didn't do. Subjects under stress have been known to manipulate the situation and do crazy things. In this situation, however, score two for police intuition!

I looked at the NCO and what he was wearing. I told him to take his right Wellington boot off and turn it upside down. He questioned me as to why I wanted him to do this. I told him I thought the bullet was in his Wellington boots and to do what I asked or I would search him myself. He complied and nothing fell out of the boot.

His commander said, "See, you are just making something out of nothing."

Then, I told the NCO to do the same with the other boot. This time he worked slower and did not turn the boot upside down. I walked over, took the boot away, and turned it over. You guessed it—the bullet fell onto the floor! The major didn't talk to any of us anymore, but he did want to leave if we were finished with his NCO. We learned later that the commander didn't do a thing to him.

I think the man got the round out while we were transporting him in the patrol unit, slid it down his pants, and the bullet eventually rested inside his boot. As we reflected upon this unpleasant episode later, we realized three valuable lessons: Trust your gut instinct/intuition, always do a proper search and seizure, and rarely trust a major.

—William "Pete" Piazza, SM sergeant, retired
air policeman, United States Air Force

The Police Sixth Sense

I am retired now, but I was a sergeant with the Ft. Lauderdale Police Department for twenty-four years. In Florida, police departments allow "off duty details." A restaurant, bar, liquor store, or other various business establishments are allowed to pay police officers directly for any extra police work they may need.

There is a major restaurant/bar called "Houston's" that hires police officers to work during their business hours. I would get off of work at the police department around 10:30 PM and then work at Houston's from 11:00 PM to 1:00 AM, twice a week. The extra $40.00 per night helped financially, and I did this for many years.

Normally, when officers worked an extra detail anywhere, they would call and inform Central Dispatch. In this particular case, I overlooked it. Most people knew, however, that there was an officer usually working at Houston's.

The restaurant closed first, and then the bar section closed at midnight. As the workers were cleaning up and closing the place down, I stuck around to make sure the place didn't get robbed as employees were leaving.

It was a hot summer night, and Houston's had a new employee in training. Before I knew it, it was 1:00 AM and time for me to leave. The business only allocated me two hours of pay and did not have the money to keep me any longer. On this night, the manager and new employee were running behind.

I made one last check in the parking lot and noticed a car parked in the lot with no one in it. I was by myself and did not have a take-home patrol car. Thus, it theoretically was more difficult for the public to know for certain whether a police officer was still working or not.

I started to walk across the parking lot to go check out this car, and for whatever reason, an inner voice told me to STOP in mid-step. The command was clear as day. I call it the "policeman's sixth sense." The voice added, "Turn around and march right back into that building."

I wasn't going to argue with the urgency. I went back into the restaurant and didn't even think about why—perhaps because I've grown to trust this voice implicitly and not question it.

I approached the manager and said "My shift has ended, do you want me to stay?"

He said, "No, that's okay, but thank you. Go on home."

I said to him, "Here are the keys. As soon as I leave out the front door, lock yourself in."

I got into my car and left.

Later, I learned that three guys armed with semi-automatic weapons were lying down in that parked car. They knew I was there when I checked them out in the lot, and they had watched me until I left. If I had walked over to the car, they would have killed me.

The manager didn't lock the front door as I suggested. The gunmen robbed the place of all the money and pistol-whipped both the manager and new girl in training. The injuries were pretty bad.

The gunmen were eventually arrested. During a post arrest interview, one gunman admitted that if I had gone over to their parked car, their plan was to shoot and kill me.

To all men and women in police work, young or veteran, please listen to that inner voice. No matter what religion you are or what you believe in, when the hair stands up on the back of your neck, pay attention to it. It means something. I had absolutely no rational reason for turning around and walking back into that restaurant, but I obeyed the command. I am alive today because of it.

—*Ted Schendel, sergeant, retired*
Ft. Lauderdale Police Department, Florida

Two Snagged for the FBI

I believe most police officers have a sixth sense that gives them the unique ability to solve a crime or to at least go in the right direction to make a case complete. During the early part of my career with the Louisiana State Police, I was assigned to Criminal Interdiction. I looked for traveling criminals, stolen cars, drug couriers, illegal aliens, or other basic violations of law on our interstate highway system. During those years, I had the unique ability to recover stolen automobiles.

On March 16, 1989, I was patrolling along eastbound on I-12 in Baton Rouge, Louisiana, when I pulled up behind a Ford truck. I was aware that this particular model of truck was one that had a high probability of being stolen. I ran a check on the Nevada tags, and not to my surprise, it was stolen.

After stopping the vehicle, we learned that it was occupied by Douglas Bennett Harper and John Paul Martin—two of the FBI's Top Ten most wanted. These two individuals were robbing post offices and stealing blank money orders. They would also steal the printers used to emboss the letters onto the blank money orders. Harper was printing checks and sending them to his common-law wife, who would cash them. We eventually put the two in jail and notified the proper federal authorities.

Fast forward one week to March 23, 1989. Again, while riding on I-12, a car licensed out of Indiana passed me and I noticed that it had no gas cap. I proceeded to stop this car, which was occupied by a male and female. After spending a few moments talking with the female driver and male passenger, my suspicions were aroused, which led me to investigate further.

I obtained a consent to search the automobile, and in the trunk were two suitcases. I opened up the female's suitcase and found a medicine bottle inside. The name on the bottle of medicine was Douglas Harper, one of the Top Ten Most Wanted. I had stopped Harper's common-law wife! She was responsible for cashing the stolen checks.

Interestingly, the first stop on the stolen truck with her common-law husband in it was on I-12 eastbound in Walker, Louisiana. The second stop on the car with no gas cap and with the common-law wife in it was I-12 westbound in Walker, Louisiana. They were in the exact same location except one was going eastbound and the other going westbound. You could have thrown a rock from stop to stop!

At that particular time, the Feds had not issued a warrant for the common-law wife's arrest, but I was able to provide information to the postal inspector to help close the case on these robberies.

These were simply two plain cars that caught my attention for some reason. Why I checked them both out is beyond me. I guess a gut feeling that something was wrong.

—Robert Landry, trooper, retired
Louisiana State Police

The Interrogation

When I first shook his hand, I knew something was wrong. He was a nice-looking, thirty-year-old man, with soft, brown eyes. However, I felt his appearance belied the truth. I could feel it, and it left me very uneasy. My inner voice was saying, "Be careful," and I called on Spirit for guidance.

A small police department asked me to interrogate him. A thirteen-year old girl was missing with no explanation other than foul play. She was an A student, loved her friends and teachers, and had no reason to run away. The man had been at her house a week prior, after having met the girl's mother at a bar. Just out of prison after a ten-year sentence, he had befriended the family, helped repair their car, and spent Saturday night at their house. A week later, after partying all night, the mother returned home and found that her daughter was missing. Police found a corner of the suspect's prison ID card stuck in the latch of the door. He said that the weekend he was there, he had demonstrated to the mother how to break into her own house if she lost her keys. I thought his explanation might be plausible to a jury, but not to me. I could tell by his handshake that something was wrong.

After hours of talking, I finally gained his trust by "getting inside his head," and he confessed to his horrific crime. He had been bar-hopping, looking for the mother. When he couldn't find her, he got mad, broke into the house, and convinced the girl that her mother needed her. The little girl didn't seem surprised, put on her shoes, and went with him wearing only her pajamas.

After he bought her a Coke at a convenience store, he wondered what he should do. He said, "I broke into the house, I am on parole, and I didn't want the little girl to tell. I had to do something to her." Eventually, he took her into the woods and killed her in ways not fit to describe. He seemed to be without feelings and totally dissociated from the event; however, he agreed to take the police to the scene.

As I was leaving, the local officers shook my hand in congratulations. Then the thought suddenly came to me, *You'd better shake his hand, too, because he's right behind you ... you could lose his trust!* I turned around and there he stood.

It had to be Spirit telling me the job wasn't complete until he led the police to her body. Though just touching him and looking again into his brown eyes gave me great distress, I responded to my inner voice.

I reached for his hand and told him very sincerely, "You're doing the right thing." I had also done the right thing.

—Ingrid P. Dean, detective sergeant, retired
Michigan State Police, Traverse City, Michigan

three

Dreams

Innovations in science and technology have been inspired by dreams and intuition, yet our culture oftentimes dismisses these avenues as legitimate ways for pursuing research or investigation. Receiving insights in these extraordinary ways can be a source of survival—our intuitive intelligence is capable of interacting with facts and situations that go beyond what is available through our five senses. In our line of police work, we utilize anything to save lives.

Dream Work

Most of my premonitions and intuitive information manifests while I'm sleeping, although sometimes I receive unusual thoughts consciously.

When I was nineteen years old and living at home, my best friend, Larry, joined the Marine Corps and was sent to Vietnam.

Even though he was a couple of years older than me, he was a lifetime friend and like a brother to me.

One night, around 2:00 AM, I thought I heard a loud knock on the door and woke up suddenly from a very sound sleep. I immediately sat up in bed and said aloud, "Larry is dead." This was unusual behavior for me. I might toss and turn or lift myself on my elbow, but never sit up in bed like that. I thought to myself, *What a stupid idea. I know Larry is okay.* Then, I lay back down and went to sleep.

The following afternoon, two Marines visited Larry's parent's home and delivered a death message. Larry had been killed in action by a mortar.

I was working as a trooper at the Flint Post. One day as I drove to work, I thought how amazing it was that with such a large population living in the city, none of the police officers had ever hit any pedestrians. At the speeds we sometimes traveled during the course of our duties, it seemed remarkable. Within two hours after the start of my shift, I was involved in a pedestrian accident. Fortunately, the person was not seriously hurt.

Many years ago, I was investigating the death of a twenty-two-year-old male. The victim lived with his parents, though he was home alone when the accident occurred. His mother returned home to find her son dead in the dining room, with a .22 caliber rifle near his body.

While conducting my investigation, I eliminated homicide as the cause of death. However, I didn't think it was a suicide either.

Not having much confidence in our Detective Bureau at the time, I did not request a detective right away. I felt the detective would write it off as a suicide. Yet, I could not figure out how his death had happened.

This case bothered me. It kept me awake. I lay in bed thinking about it. I could not let this nice family believe their son had deliberately killed himself if he had not. Finally, one night I fell into a restless sleep. In my dreams, I reviewed my interview notes and revisited the scene. I analyzed and assessed the information I had over and over again in my mind—even though I was in a dream-like state. Suddenly, I awakened. I knew what had happened.

When I went to work the next day, my shift sergeant suggested I talk to a detective, just to protect myself from legal responsibility. I chose the detective I had the most confidence in and told him what I believed happened. After I told him my theory, I went to the autopsy while the shift sergeant went back to the scene to check it out.

I believed that the victim, while his mother was gone, started cleaning his .22 caliber rifle. One of his brothers told me the weapon occasionally jammed, and a round could be left in the gun. The dining room had a wooden circular chandelier. I believe the victim held the weapon up to the light from the chandelier to check the barrel for cleanliness. He probably held the feeder latch open with his thumb. Then, he accidentally struck the chandelier with the butt of the rifle, his finger slipped off the latch, and the latch fell shut. With a jammed round left in the weapon, the weapon went off and struck the victim in the heart.

The detective confirmed this theory by locating an indentation in the wooden chandelier. It matched the edge of the butt of the gun. There was also some varnish on the butt of the gun from the wood of the chandelier. As confirmed in the autopsy, the angle of the wound through the heart was the exact angle that proved my theory. I solved the mystery while I was asleep.

—*Lawrence A. Bak, sergeant*
Michigan State Police, Alpena, Michigan

Dream Warning

Police work seems to attract young men who have big egos and want to be macho. In Recruit School, the cadets think they know everything. They show off their genitalia, belch, burp, and fart in the classroom (only when the instructor leaves the room, of course). I was one of these guys, and I thought I was so smart. Because I'd shot rifles and shotguns ever since I was a kid, I thought I knew all about handguns, too.

After one particularly stressful ten-hour day of lectures and classes on defensive tactics and lifesaving techniques, running, and shooting on the range—I was tired. It seems when I'm tired, I dream a lot. The dream I had that night concerned my pistol, which I had received just two days before.

I have returned to my elementary school and am in the classroom of one of my favorite teachers. I tell the teacher, "I'm here, policing at the school now. I'm here to guard the kids."

As I'm walking the hallways, a gangbanger sneaks into the school and I hear a commotion coming from my former teacher's classroom. I run into the room and pull out my handgun as I see the robber trying to take off with the teacher's money. Unfortunately, my gun falls apart, right in my hand! I am embarrassed. I can't believe this is happening in front of my role-model teacher. The gangbanger escapes through a window while mooning the class.

I wake up thinking, *Damn! Some cop I am!* The next day, I am tired but prepared for early morning hallway inspection. This is when all the recruits stand at attention next to the door of their bedrooms while police instructors stop in front of each recruit to inspect them. We know "inspection" is a game. Most of us never take anything personally. Instructors like to yell at you, just to see if you can take it. We simply deal with it.

So, I'm standing by my door with my pistol in my right hand, both arms hanging by my sides. The rule is, as soon the instructor turns to face you, your right hand comes straight up from the elbow, so that your weapon is pointing straight up. The goal is to be sharp and quick about it.

Our new guns are Sig Sauer 9mm handguns. I had cleaned mine the night before. Cleaning requires taking it completely apart, dousing it with gun cleaner, brushing it, wiping it, pulling a rod and pad through it, applying oil, and then putting it back together again. No big deal. I had cleaned long guns all my life.

As soon as the instructor faces me, my elbow goes up (quickly and sharply, I might add). In one split-second jerk, the slide flies off like an elongated bullet and hits the instructor square in the nuts! *Oops.* I cringe. My fellow peers are snickering.

The whole friggin' gun falls apart! Every itty-bitty piece tumbles to the floor.

The instructor grabs his groin and I realize my dream has come true. I have embarrassed myself in front of one of my favorite instructors. I wasn't feeling macho anymore. I had forgotten to lock one simple part.

My dream had warned me, but I didn't listen. And, I soon realized my nightmare had just begun—I did push-ups for the remainder of Recruit School.

—L.L. Bean, detective sergeant
Michigan State Police, Detroit, Michigan

A Mother's Dream

In March 2004, the Manistique Public Safety Department went through a huge upheaval due to financial difficulties experienced by the City of Manistique. One officer got laid off, the director was forced to retire, and our full-time dispatcher/clerk was cut back to four hours a day. This meant that our full-time department of ten personnel lost twenty-five percent of its workforce. Although my position was still that of sergeant, my title was now the acting director of Manistique Public Safety.

One of our desires, as a department, was to change our uniforms. The current uniforms—light-blue shirts with French-blue pants—were outdated. We never wore ties, except for court appearances. The uniform looked sloppy. After polling the officers, we unanimously voted to change to a dark-blue uniform—LAPD style. The officers even agreed to purchase the uniforms with their own money.

The new uniforms arrived in time for the annual July Fourth parade and festivities in Manistique. As the commanding officer of our department, it was my duty to lead the parade.

After dressing in the new uniform that morning, I looked in the mirror and was impressed with the way I looked. Then I remembered a dream my mother had told me about.

My mother died in 1995. Throughout my childhood, my sister, father, and I were continually astounded by her dreams, as many of them often came true.

In 1976, I graduated from college with a bachelor's degree in criminal justice. After working for several small departments, I joined the Manistique Public Safety Department in 1978, because it was a chance to move back to my hometown. Although I accepted the position, I did not want to stay in Manistique forever and was continually applying to larger departments, including the Michigan State Police. In fact, there were many times I longed to quit my position in Manistique. I always hoped that a dream job would open up—and I was given many other opportunities—the trouble was I could not make up my mind about where to go.

In 1985, I was accepted by the Michigan State Police and started to make preparations to quit Manistique and enter the State Police Academy. I was not thoroughly convinced that this was a good move, however, and was torn about what to do (I also had another job offer pending with a sheriff's department). My job situation was causing me a lot of personal turmoil. To make matters more confusing, my boss advised me that if I stayed in Manistique, they were going to give me a detective's position within the department, and this was something I really wanted.

At the peak of my frustration, I stopped to see my mother for coffee. I had always been close to her and often used her as a sounding board and source of advice, therefore, she was aware of my current dilemma. She told me that she had a dream about my job problem that she wanted to tell me about.

In her dream, she saw me standing at attention with a group of officers. She said something was going on; there was a big "doing," like a parade or something. I immediately asked Mom where this was happening. She replied that it was in Manistique, though she did not know where. I then asked her what color uniform I was wearing. She replied, "Dark blue." I was relieved because I thought it meant I would become a member of the Michigan State Police and be stationed in Manistique in the future. I said, "I'm with the state police, right?"

"No, not the state police," Mom said. "I know their uniforms and it is not theirs." My mother knew all of the uniforms well because my father ran a wrecker service, and Mom was his secretary. City police, state police, and sheriff officers visited their repair shop frequently. I pressed her for more details.

She stated again that the event was in town and we were standing at attention and looked very proud. She also said I was the leader of the men and that our uniforms were dark blue, including the shirts, pants, and ties.

I just shook my head. I was absolutely certain Mom was wrong on this one—there was no way this dream could become true. Manistique Public Safety wore light-blue uniforms, and she had said I was not with the state police. I told Mom she was wrong this time.

She looked at me, smiled, and shook her bony finger at me. "You'll see. This was a very strong dream. It will come true," she predicted.

As I stood in front of the mirror that morning, I realized Mom's dream, which she'd had so many years ago, had validity.

—*Kenneth C. Golat, chief of police*
Manistique Department of Public Safety, Manistique, Michigan

A Clairvoyant Dream

On September 11, 2001, I woke up and went for a walk with my sister in the early morning hours. We both wanted to get in better shape, so we power-walked around the Civic Center track. I was tired and straggled behind her. "I'm so sorry," I said, "but I had this awful dream last night. When I woke up, I was just *exhausted!*" Since we always told our dreams to each other, I proceeded to tell her about mine.

I was in the middle of a revolution. I was in a war. I think a bomb was dropped on us. I was with all these people I didn't know. We were running, and then we stopped. We just huddled together in this building. It was so dark. Parts of the building were falling all around us. There was smoke and fire everywhere, and I couldn't breathe. I was gasping for air. We ran down the stairs but were suddenly stopped. We were trapped, with no way out. It was horrible. I knew I was going to die—and I gave up!

"I've never had a dream like this before," I told her.

My sister listened attentively, and as we finished up our walk, we tried to interpret the dream. Neither of us could imagine what it meant. We both thought maybe I had remembered an event from another lifetime.

When I arrived at work at eight, I wrote an e-mail to a friend downstate. I told him about my dream. I just couldn't let go of it. It was so unsettling. I had no sooner sent the e-mail when my partner came into my office. He was agitated and said, "An airplane has just crashed into one of the Twin Towers!"

I thought little of it. It was probably a student pilot that went off course and somehow hit the building.

About twenty minutes later, my partner ran into my office again, this time distraught. He gasped, "Another plane just crashed into the other building! They are *airliners!* I think we're being attacked!"

My heart fell to the floor and my stomach turned over as I remembered my dream from last night. I hurried to the conference room where everyone was watching the TV, and saw the smoke and the fire spewing out of the buildings.

The room was silent. No one uttered a word. I started shaking my head, nearly crying, and blurted, "The buildings are both going to fall down. There are thousands of people still inside them!" We were all sick to our stomachs. We stood there, watching as the buildings came down. It was awful.

I believe there is a connection between all policemen. We have the same mission—to help others. We are a family. We feel the excitement and the pain of our brothers. I think, somehow, I tuned into my police family when I had that dream. I felt their distress and I lived some of the chaos with them before it happened. What disturbed me most was meeting death and accepting its inevitability.

That day, hundreds of policemen and rescue workers died. Ultimately, it affected the country and the whole world. The profound importance to our national and global life must have been a factor that triggered my vision.

I wonder how a person can move out of the confines of time and live a few moments in the future. I don't have the answers—but I know I was there.

—A. A. Seller, detective sergeant
Michigan State Police, Detroit, Michigan

four
Ghostly Apparitions & Haunted Effects

People have claimed to have encounters with spirits in visible form for eons, yet ghostly apparitions have always been difficult to explain. We may never know for certain what they are and where they come from, but the intense and assorted emotions they evoke are undeniably real. While some evidence concerning the existence of ghosts is extremely compelling—especially now that we have video and photography available in the modern era—still, many scientists and other professionals are not convinced. Some believe, for instance, that witnesses are just "matrixing" or "anthropomorphizing" such encounters. Interestingly, police officers are not, generally, anthropomorphic people. Thus, their ghost stories are undeniably persuasive and gripping!

Not Human

One night, while doing property inspections in back of the Ryan Elementary School in Bronson, Michigan, I went back to the athletic building, which is about 100 yards from the school. Red flags surrounded the building, which prevented me from driving around it. I parked my patrol car facing the building and left the headlights and spot light on.

When I walked up to the southeast corner, I observed lights going out. I figured this was the large light in front of the building. One to three seconds after the lights went out, I stepped from the corner, and observed my patrol car lights were out.

I drew my weapon and walked toward the patrol car. I knew whoever turned the lights off had to be in the patrol car. After walking up to the car, I cleared the front seat and back seat. No one was in the patrol car. I figured it had to be a short in the wiring. I got into the patrol car and then observed the head light switch was turned off.

It is impossible for anybody to have turned the lights off. I did not hear or see a car door open or close, and I was only twenty yards from the patrol car. This scared the crap out of me!

I went back to the department and advised the chief of the incident. I asked him if he could give me a logical explanation. The chief advised that he could not.

Time of incident: 0300 hours on a clear summer night. Whatever turned the lights off was not human!

—*Chip Hovarter, officer*
Bronson Police Department, Bronson, Michigan

Her Voice

When I first heard the woman's voice, I had been involved in the thirty-five-year-old investigation for eight years. This particular cold case involved the murder of a twenty-three-year-old college student in 1969. Like so many others, this one had been shelved time after time over the years due to a lack of investigative leads. It was the kind of case that every police department has—the one referred to as *the case*—and everyone knows which one you are talking about.

Finally, after years of dead-ends, science might come to our rescue. Breakthrough DNA-extraction technology had just become available, and evidence from the case had been delivered to the lab for analysis. There was nothing left for us to do at this point but to wait patiently for the results. We desperately hoped for a break in the case.

During this time, I traveled to Baton Rouge, Louisiana, to attend an FBI-sponsored violent crimes seminar. While there, I spoke to several of my counterparts at length, explaining what our scientists were attempting to do with the evidence. I was also fishing for any investigative ideas they might have.

After many hours of exchanging tall-tales and war stories, I went back to my hotel room and in the early morning hours, I quickly fell asleep—or so I thought. After what seemed like only minutes, I distinctly heard a female voice softly calling my name. As I hovered in that familiar valley between sleep and conscious thought, the voice continued to slowly call my name: "Adam, wake up. I need you." The voice seemed to be getting closer, increasing in volume and clarity, until I knew I was fully awake. As I lay there, trying to understand what I thought was a strange dream, I once again heard her voice urgently calling my name and telling me to wake up—I was needed.

The voice was so clear and so close—it was right next to me! I could feel her breath on my neck! This realization startled me and I instantly jumped out of bed and fumbled for the light switch. I thought, *maybe someone is playing a trick on me and is hiding in the room.*

Upon turning on the lights I saw no one. I searched the entire room, including the closet, bathroom, and behind the TV. I even opened the door to check the hallway for stragglers—all to no avail. I was alone.

Needless to say it took me quite awhile to fall asleep after this scare. Eventually, I chalked it up to being a bad dream from sleeping in a strange bed...until I returned home.

On the following Monday, as I sat in a meeting sipping coffee and listening halfheartedly to the speaker, I received a 911 page from the lab. Could this be what we've been waiting for all these years? I excused myself from the room and immediately called the lab. They had a positive Combined DNA Index System (CODIS) notification! Score one for the scientists! They had identified the person responsible for this crime. By analyzing the offender's DNA that was embedded into the weave of the victim's clothing, and matching that DNA profile to a list of known felons, the lab was able to give us a name. We could now move the investigation forward and bring it to a successful conclusion.

Although I have never believed in ghosts or the paranormal, I am unable to provide any earthly explanation for what

I experienced in that hotel room. I believe it was the victim calling to me and telling me I was needed. Her message of "Adam, wake up—I need you" is etched firmly in my mind. I can still hear her voice and feel her breath on my neck. She knew it was time for me to wake up; that things were happening that needed my attention. She was right.

—*A. Miller, detective sergeant*
Michigan State Police, Lansing, Michigan

Pushed and Saved!

It was just about quitting time on a cold December 5 afternoon. I always got an anxious feeling in the pit of my stomach at quitting time, because I worried that the dispatchers would conjure up something special to assign me at the last possible minute. All I had on my mind was picking up my one- and five-year-old boys and getting home to where it was comfy cozy. I was tired of being out in the cold air all day and had evil thoughts about turning off, or at least turning down the police radio so I could later claim that I didn't hear any last minute radio calls. But I laughed at myself and left the radio to proclaim its endless parade of police calls.

As sure as the sun sets, I received a radio call of a suspicious vehicle. The occupants of the vehicle had open containers of beer when they stopped in a bank drive-thru. As soon as I acknowledged the radio call, this very same suspicious vehicle drove by me. I couldn't believe it! Darn it! I couldn't ignore it.

I conducted a standard police traffic stop several blocks away from where I first spotted this vehicle and in front of the local hospital where my wife was presently working. I cautiously walked up to the car and saw closed containers of beer still in the store paper sack and situated on the floorboard in front of the passenger. There was no aroma of beer, and the two adults and a very small child, who were in the vehicle, seemed pleasant and mild mannered.

I checked the driver's license, and I checked for warrants. All checked out okay until I noticed that the license plates had expired. I explained to the driver that the vehicle would have to be towed and he would receive a citation for the expired plates. I told him to have a seat in the back of my cruiser, and that I'd explain how to take care of everything and all would be okay. He complied without incident. My shift supervisor arrived and kept watch over the other occupants.

I got in the driver seat of the cruiser with the driver of the stopped vehicle seated behind me. It all happened so fast that to this day I cannot properly articulate what happened next—I just know it happened.

As I explained to the driver the procedure for getting his car out of impound, the hairs on the back of my neck felt tingly. In the blink of an eye, it seemed, I felt a very strong urging, a prompting to "Get out!" "Get out!" This strong prompting felt like a sense of dire urgency that danger was fast approaching and to "Get out!" It was as if some unknown entity was very strongly trying to nudge me quickly out of the cruiser. I felt it, but it wasn't like how a human physically pushes another human. It's like an internal *feeling* of being pushed and of someone telling you to "Get out!" No actual voice, but a feeling of someone speaking. It's very difficult to explain.

I very rapidly got out of the cruiser. As I got out, this "feeling" prompted me to draw my firearm and confront the driver. After I jerked open the rear door of the cruiser, my jaw dropped. I could plainly see him raising a handgun from between his legs and pointing it at the back of the driver's seat where I was seated! I must have gotten out of the cruiser and drew my weapon so fast that it took him by surprise.

My supervisor and I wrestled the gun from the driver, and he was arrested on a felony charge. The suspect's gun was loaded with 9 mm rounds, and there was one in the chamber. I learned my lesson, and I frisk whoever gets in the cruiser—with some exceptions—and I listen to my intuition, or to whatever entity might be trying to help me.

I had other incidents in my career involving these strong urgings or promptings—an interior "voice" if you will—that led to the recovery of murdered people. I never mentioned these incidents before, because no one wants to be labeled "crazy"—especially a police officer.

—Michael G. DeVita, patrolman, retired
Lima Police Department, Lima, Ohio

Spirits of the North
Excerpt from the book
Alaska Behind Blue Eyes by Alan L. White.

I've never been what you might call "poltergeist inclined." I enjoy a good horror movie as much as the next person, but I always dismissed alleged true tales of wandering spirits as figments of people's overactive imaginations. I always believed each strange occurrence had at least one logical explanation. This was, of course, before I began working the late-night shift in City Hall at Skagway, Alaska.

Skagway's City Hall and police department are housed in the McCabe College Building. The local court, the magistrate's office, and Trail of 98 Museum also share the space. This grand old structure was built in 1900 as a woman's college and was, for a time, the only granite building in Alaska.

As with any old building, it had the obligatory creaks, groans, and murmurs. Unfortunately, no one bothered to tell me it was haunted. I say this now with some certainty, even though it may damage any reputation I have left as being a practical man.

After a break-in period, my first duty assignment was working the midnight shift. Sitting in the office during the wee hours, I would occasionally hear a few strange noises, but I never gave them much thought. One early morning incident, however, changed my perception of what goes bump in the night—forever.

I was working at my desk on some much-neglected paperwork. The building was silent except for the faint hum of the Macintosh computer and my fingers performing a slow dance on the keyboard. Fighting off sleepiness caused by a daytime person trying to be nocturnal, I struggled with a rather boring theft report.

I had nearly completed the narrative when I heard a door close. The door was in a rear hallway off of the court chambers. I recognized this door because of the many times I'd heard it close before. It was attached to a police storage room where uniforms and other equipment were kept. The solid oak door was at least two inches thick. An ancient brass knob and lock-set hinted at its age. The door would not stay open on its own and, if not held, would quickly slam shut behind you. As the door was swinging it made the most hideous screeching sound.

After hearing the door close, my first thought was, *Maybe someone is in, or has been in, the storage room.* This idea was quickly dismissed because the entire building was dark when I arrived. My second thought was, *Maybe someone left the door propped open and whatever was holding it gave way.*

I wasn't the least bit nervous as I rose from the desk and confidently walked through the dark courtroom and into the even darker hallway. After some fumbling around I turned on the hall light and approached the storage room door. I pulled on the knob and found it properly latched. Upon opening the door, the equipment room was dark, as it should be. I turned on the light and all of the contents seemed to be in order. I turned off the light and let the door shut on its own, with the loud screeching and confident slam. Before walking away, I pulled on the knob one more time. It was locked.

Satisfied, I returned to my desk and began making finishing touches to the report.

A few minutes later, I again heard the loud screech and the finality of the door slamming shut. This made the hair on the back of my neck rise to attention. Spooks were not on my mind at this point. I knew SOMEONE must have opened the door.

I pulled my weapon and made my way back to the dark courtroom, using my best "there-might-be-a-bad-guy-on-the premises" stalking maneuvers.

I listened for signs of an intruder. As I crouched outside the door, all was silent in the hallway. My left hand reached for the light switch and the bulb snapped on. I pounced forward, gun pointing down the hall, prepared for whoever was breaking in or out. The hallway was empty. It then occurred to me that whoever opened the door must be hiding in the storage room. Using the before-mentioned police maneuvers, I opened the storage room door. No one was there.

I carefully looked around the assorted boxes and racks until I felt satisfied that I was, in fact, alone. Somewhat relieved, I stepped back into the hallway and secured my weapon. I opened and closed the door several times, performing the "this can't be happening" test. Each time the door securely latched and held. I even tried leaving the door shut and unlatched, and discovered that it would stay resting against the casing. Then, shutting the door with a forceful push, I pulled the knob as hard as I dared, making sure it was properly latched. I returned to my desk, feeling confident all was in order. As I settled into my chair, the door screeched. This time, I was scared. My previous search had confirmed that no *living* being was stalking City Hall, which left only one possible explanation. Since the door could not have opened by itself, some *thing* had caused this to happen.

Ever so slowly, I walked toward the hallway, with my gun secured. Whatever was opening the door would not be stopped by bullets. The door was, of course, closed and securely latched.

I stood in the hallway for awhile, carefully listening and watching for signs of movement. Nothing happened.

By this time, completing the report was the last thing on my mind, but I decided to finish the task. All was quiet as I returned to my desk. I sat stiffly in the chair, determined to not be chased from the building. Minutes ticked by as I waited for the next occurrence.

All right, I thought, *if some sort of supernatural phenomenon is going on here, it will have to deal with me. I will not be run off by some annoying spirit held over from the Klondike era. Not Alan White, no sir!*

You might say my sitting and listening while encamped behind the desk was admirable; after awhile, though, it became boring. I was about to write the whole episode off to midnight shifts, when the door screeched shut. Once again, I got the familiar feeling of hair leaping to attention on my neck; however, it was not as bad this time.

Is that the best you can do? I smugly thought. *What's to closing a door? Any old spirit can handle that, you two-bit piece of suspended animation!* As I considered additional insults, a two-bit something began to walk across the creaky wooden floor of the museum above me. I was familiar with the sound. I thought this new noise might be a result of my overactive imagination, but the footsteps were, well, *hauntingly real.*

When my heartbeat slowed to a reasonable level, I studied the new sound. Definite footsteps could be heard crossing the floor from east to west. They would stop for a time, and then return to where they had begun. Having no intention of going up to the museum, I chose to remain at my desk, in a cold sweat. The door screeched again. I threw up my hands in disgust.

Great, this is all I need! Everyone thought I was nuts for coming to Alaska in the first place, and now I find myself in a haunted department. I sat in my chair for another half hour, listening to the supernatural activities. Then anger set in. *I didn't need this. What had I done to deserve this phenomenon?* I was now totally disgusted.

The door shut again. I jumped from my chair, just as whatever was walking around upstairs bumped into something. I began my first attempt at ghost-busting. "Now, knock it off!" I yelled as loudly as I could. The sound of my voice startled me and, apparently, the spirits moving about were startled, too. There was absolute silence.

Ha! They're intimidated by me! I thought. Then continuing my tirade, I strutted around the room. "I did not travel over three thousand miles to be haunted! Why don't you guys, or girls, or whatever, find some other building to run amuck in? Hey you, upstairs! You bump into something? Good! I hope you stubbed your, ah ... thing! Now, go back to wherever you go during the day and leave me alone! You're really starting to tick me off!"

Returning to my chair, I enjoyed the new peace and quiet. My fit seemed to have worked.

Later in my shift, I went back out on patrol, feeling rather good about myself. *Told them a thing or two,* I smugly thought as I drove down Broadway and checked out a few buildings.

Larry relieved me at the shift change, but I said nothing about ghostly wanderings. A bright sunny day had dawned and now it all seemed like a dream. Besides, I wasn't sure I wanted to share an experience like this. I had no idea how common it was for someone who carried a weapon for a living to experience strange night moves.

Luckily, the City Hall spirits left me alone—most of the time. Every few weeks though, the midnight shift would get weird. After listening for awhile, I would yell, "Knock it off!" And all would be quiet for the rest of the night. I became so used to this procedure that I started to be rather matter-of-fact about it.

On one of the few days Larry and I had off together, we were sitting in his living room. "Hey Larry," I asked, "you ever hear anything, you know, *strange*, when you're working in the office late at night?"

The look on his face was telling. "What do you mean when you say *strange*?" Larry asked, choosing his words carefully.

"Ah, you know, doors closing, footsteps overhead in the museum, that sort of thing."

"Oh, thank you," Larry sighed. "I thought I was going insane or something."

Larry and I discussed the situation for some time.

"Just yell 'Knock it off!'" I said, feeling like an old pro. "They hate that."

—*Alan L. White, patrol officer*
Clare Police Department, Clare, Michigan

The Bowers Harbor Inn

My partner and I were working the midnight shift. It was a cloudy, windy night. He was telling me about an encounter that he and another officer had with our local haunted restaurant, the Bowers Harbor Inn. The fact that we were driving on a stretch of road on a peninsula that was directly across from the restaurant reminded him of the story.

In the middle of his monologue, Central Dispatch called for available units to respond to an alarm—at the Bowers Harbor Inn! We were the closest unit, so, of course, we responded.

When we arrived at the restaurant, my partner went around one side of the building and I went around the other. I noticed a stairway leading up to a door on the second floor. I climbed the stairs to check the door. When I turned the handle, the door opened. I gently pulled the door closed so that it rested on the casing—but it wasn't completely shut. I notified my partner that I had discovered an open door.

When the key holder arrived, he let us into the building. My partner and I cleared the first floor of the restaurant and then proceeded to the second floor. When we reached the door I had left open, it was completely shut and *locked*! In order to open the door again, we had to use the key.

There was nobody in the building.

—Dawn Wagoner, detective
Grand Traverse Sheriff Department, Traverse City, Michigan

MSP Patrol Car 12-8: Haunted or Blessed?

I am a graduate of the Michigan State Police 98th Recruit School, assigned to my first post at Brighton—Post #12. In 1986, I was eastbound on I-96, running radar to clock westbound traffic. I clocked a gray Corvette at 93 mph in a 70 mph zone. Nothing really too uncommon, just a fast speeder in this area sometimes.

At the time, I was driving Michigan State Police (MSP) patrol car 12-8, a slick top. I cut the median and made my turn to go west after the vehicle. The Corvette then made a run for it. It appeared that the driver decided he was not going to get a ticket, and I kicked 12-8 to the floor. The chase was on!

Most MSP veterans recall the 1985 the Dodge/Plymouth patrol cars, which had the 318 cubic inch engine and four barrel carburetors. Top speed on a good day was probably 110 mph. Those were the days.

I pursued this vehicle, and other traffic was pulling to the right shoulder as the Corvette blew by them. As I continued, I watched people checking their mirrors so that no one pulled in front of me as I kept 12-8 to the floor, trying to make up ground. The Corvette had to slow down now and then, as traffic was in its way. This gave me the opportunity to close the gap. I traveled as fast as the car would go up the grade at approximately 105 mph.

Vehicle traffic was still pulling to the right to keep the path clear. I entered onto the Grand River overpass and a vehicle changed lanes, right to left. I got clipped. 12-8 began to go to the left. I never struck the overpass or another vehicle from this point.

Everything went white and I didn't feel any motion. It was the strangest space to be in. After I stopped and my senses returned, I was in the middle of westbound I-96 facing east. My mind was blank. Many people stopped and came to the patrol car. The only real words I heard were, "are you alright?" I just felt "out there," and thought to myself, *I'm still here! How can this be?*

Once I was out of the patrol car, I looked at all the skids on the freeway from 12-8. All the skids and spin marks were going down the center of west I-96 and showed the patrol car spinning for a long distance. The grass median was to the south. If I had hit the median, I would have tumbled and rolled and undoubtedly been killed.

There was a partial guardrail to the right. If I'd hit the guardrail, or missed it going off the roadway, I certainly I would have been killed. I have no sense of hitting the brake or gas pedal as I spun around. Everything just went white!

Patrol car 12-8 was damaged from the impact. Its wheels were bent in on the left side, but the car did not roll. Nor did the tires break their beads, which would have caused them to go flat. I escaped a rollover—thank goodness! The car definitely had to go to the body shop for repair, however.

Two letters came to the post regarding this accident. Both parties wrote letters stating what a tremendous job of driving I did, and that I probably would not have survived if I had left the roadway. If the truth be told, I wasn't driving! I was definitely elsewhere, but where? I still can't figure it out to this day. I didn't pass out. Was this Divine intervention happening?

MSP car 12-8 was repaired and put back into service, but it continuously broke down. We couldn't keep it on the road due to one mishap after the other. It was not a high mileage car either. I admit, after what I went through, I was a bit spooked to drive it, because it kept breaking down.

Later that year, I was transferred to the Detroit Post. I was informed that car 12-8, due to all the problems it was having, was turned in early.

Car 12-8 did all that spinning down the center of west I-96 and never struck another car ahead of me. Was it luck? God? Why didn't I go into the median? I faintly remember a voice telling me in my head, "No, Harold, not now." I'll never be able to explain the "white" I saw.

I find the numbers of the car 12-8 quite intriguing. It was my first patrol car accident. Just prior to my retirement, I was assigned a new car, a slick top 76-2. The car had 1,200 miles on it when I hit a deer. That was my second accident in a slick top patrol car, so now have 1-2. My call sign is 76-8. Add them together and the number 12-8 keeps coming up.

Numbers are a funny thing.

—*Harold Falan, trooper, retired*
Michigan State Police, Cadillac, Michigan

Murder Suspect Confesses

Once I did a polygraph test on a murder suspect. I tried everything to get a confession. After a couple of hours, I was fixing to let the deputy take him back to jail. I left the murder suspect with the thought that the spirit of the murdered victim would not rest until closure was made on her case. Later that evening, the suspect woke up screaming. He claimed the spirit of the woman he killed was after him. He confessed that night in order to get peace from the spirit beyond.

—*Robert Landry, trooper, retired*
Louisiana State Police, Gonzales, Louisiana

Mukwa Moosa

My family lived in a small resort town in northern Michigan during the 1970s. Our home was fairly close to the downtown area, so we always had visitors and unexpected company. Often, the visitors were people who traveled from town to town, and they would be hungry or in need of a place to sleep. My mother always accommodated them as long as they didn't drink alcohol or show up at our place drunk.

I would listen to the conversations that my elders and visitors would have at the dinner table. Many of the conversations included lots of laughter and reminiscing about the "good ol' days." Other conversations were about how they survived the Catholic Holy Childhood Indian Boarding School in Harbor Springs, Michigan, and the harsh and abusive experiences they had from the nuns and priests. However, some conversations were even more serious and had to do with Indian legends and older ways of life. These stories were passed along as gospel and never joked about. They were only shared with other native families—never with whites or non-Indians.

There is one such story that always scared everyone and was never told at night when the spirits are active—the story of *Mukwa Moosa,* or the "Bearwalk,"is only passed on with the utmost respect. The legend explains that certain gifted Native American people practice either "good medicine" or "bad medicine." Good medicine equates to a pure, wholesome way of life, honoring our Creator, God. Bad medicine is the opposite way of life and entails wickedness, evil, and bad intentions. Death always lingers nearby with bad medicine.

These gifted people have the ability, when taught, to change themselves and their physical being into any animal of their choosing. I was told they could change themselves into a bear, deer, bird, or even an insect if they desired. They could also change themselves into a ball of light—an "orb," as some people call them today. The "orbs" were known to travel along a path, a roadway, or a shoreline (among other places), and to follow their paths slowly and methodically—slightly off the ground in a levitated state.

Native elders told me that it is bad luck to see one of the "Bearwalks." They believe the orbs are seen whenever an evil spell is cast upon someone for some reason. It was never explained to me if the person casting the spell was living or dead. I later came to the opinion that it didn't matter. I learned that this Bearwalk is still very much alive today and that the dead still use this spell at their leisure. I realized this from my own experience.

I am a deputy for the local sheriff's department in Traverse City, Michigan. One night while I was out on patrol, alone, I stopped at this local cemetery, which has a horseshoe driveway with two points of entry or exit. I had been stopping at this cemetery for years, but always in the daytime. Once inside the cemetery, heavy tree and brush growth could conceal a fully marked patrol car from the roadway. I could take a break to adjust my duty belt, vest, and tuck in my shirt—all without being seen by passing motorists.

It was night when I stopped for such a break and had planned to continue on my way. I parked in the same place I always parked. As I was adjusting my uniform (my duty belt was still off and laying on the trunk of my car), I looked to the north and saw an object that was very unforgettable. There, about twenty feet from me, was a ball of light radiating in a dull glow and elevated off the ground! It was about twenty- four inches off the ground and was slowly moving to the west around the headstones in the cemetery.

The ball of light glowed but there were no beams of light protruding from the surface. It seemed to be about the size of a basketball, perhaps slightly smaller. Within seconds, I started to rationalize and make sense of it—like all police officers do. I thought that maybe a car was on the road nearby, traveling north, and that the glow was a reflection of the headlights from the smooth side of a headstone. I looked to the south and there were no cars at all. I was the only one in the cemetery—this spirit, which I had only heard about as a kid, and me.

The light continued to move to the west at a slow rate and near the headstones in the cemetery. There was no noise associated with the movement, only the sound of my heartbeat as the hair on my neck and back stood straight up. I was close enough to touch it if I had elected to walk the short distance, but that option never entered my mind.

Seconds later, I knew exactly what I was seeing. It was *Mukwa Moosa*, or the "Bearwalker," that I had heard about years before. In fear now, I quickly put myself together and left the cemetery. I never looked back as I drove away, so I don't know where it went. My presumption was that it had come from underground, from a particular burial lot or casket of a native person who was interned there. I thought it had been sent to warn me, to scare me, and to remind me that I was standing on hallowed ground.

The next day, I drove to the township building where the cemetery records are kept and asked the township clerk if I could review the records. I hoped that I would recognize a last name in the burial records, which might make sense of what I had witnessed. I reviewed approximately 190 names and none of them were Native American. I could only rationalize that perhaps this ball of light was a woman who married and had her name changed, and that her husband or she was buried in this cemetery.

It was at that time that a township clerk told me about a $1.00 recording fee imposed by the township at the turn of the century, and that people had to pay this fee in order to be added to the ledger. Many of the farmers, lumberjacks, natives, locals, and poor people could not afford the fee. Consequently, there were many people who were buried in the cemetery but not recorded on the ledger. Their names and origins are unknown. Certainly, unnamed graves exist at this old cemetery.

Several months passed and I was able to tell the story to my great uncle. He was in his eighties—a traditional native elder who still spoke the tribal language. He follows the old way—the traditional path—or the "red road" as some people call it. I asked for his interpretation of my ordeal. He only laughed and answered me with this story:

I was a kid, living in Petoskey. My friends and I were playing by the lake along the railroad grade. It was getting close to dark when several of the boys and I saw a ball of light traveling along the railroad tracks. We stopped, and feeling fearless, started throwing rocks at the Bearwalk. One of the boys hit the orb and it dropped immediately to the ground. In great fear, we ran to our homes. I told my mother about what we saw. My mother consoled me as she talked about a certain local native elder who had been practicing bad medicine. She told me his name. Several days later, I was walking along the street in downtown Petoskey and saw the Indian man my mother had named. The man had a fresh wound on his forehead above one eye.

It took years for this story to escape my family social circle. I only talked about it to native people because they would be the only people who understood it. I didn't think it would be wise to mention it to fellow police officers at work.

I have struggled with spirituality for years and my law enforcement career does not make it any easier. I have tried to find a church, for instance, that my family and I would be comfortable with, but I haven't been successful. Two things are clear in my mind, however, after having lived this experience—there is a God and spirits walk among us.

A cemetery is a place of peace, tranquility, and harmony. It is hallowed ground and needs to be highly respected. Remember that when you enter a cemetery, the door to another dimension is already open to you! Walk in peace.

—*Scott Schwander, deputy*
Grand Traverse Sheriff Department, Traverse City, Michigan

War Burial

We were protecting twenty-eight nuclear bombs, all but four of which were in storage in a 300 x 200-meter restricted area. The other four were attached to fighter/bombers in an Alert Pad commanded by Colonel Chuck Yeager. In his autobiography, *Yeager* (on page 288 hardcover, and on page 367 soft cover), he mentions our base and mission, and how ready he was to use us on Red China if they planned to send portions of their 20-million-man standing army into Vietnam to wipe our guys off the earth. It was a giant chess game.

We had to contend with an invasion by a group of soldiers only 81 miles away, and we didn't have ANY fresh air to breathe several nights a week, thanks to an unfiltered crematory located less than a mile away. The fog was so thick at night that a flashlight was good for only 15 inches (to protect 300 meters). Perimeter light bulbs were made locally and not sealed against moisture. There were forty species of snakes, of which all but one was toxic and two were sea snakes. We were not allowed to shoot them, and we had no bayonets or anti-venom kits.

One night in the storage area (officially, MMS), I was on one 300-meter post. Another fellow from my "flight" (shift) was on the parallel post, but 200 meters apart. Our supervisor had already passed by, checking various posts, and the area supervisor for MMS was inside the gate shack at the Entry Control Point.

This airman MP, near one end of his post, in the forming fog, saw two glowing orbs about eye level. He thought it was his imagination or exhaustion (we only got 2.5 hours of sleep a day, on average), so he turned and walked farther toward the end of the post when something suddenly tapped his shoulder. He turned and saw the two orbs right in front of his face! He droped his M-16 and ran off post (two "no-nos"), and he never performed his duties again. After a psychological evaluation at Clark Air Base, he received a medical discharge for fear. I didn't see anything that night.

About two weeks later, however, USAF officials had arranged to have local farmers come into a cordoned off area inside the restricted area to deepen and widen the woefully inadequate drainage ditches. They were supposed to line them with concrete stones. I started work on a day shift at the same post I'd been at the other night. The farmers started their work, but suddenly dropped all their tools and ran out of the area. I went over to look.

They had unearthed the coffin of a WWII Japanese officer, which was buried six inches under the soil surface in a "Priority A USAF facility!" For twenty-five years, no one had known it was there. Our base had been a start-off point for Japanese Zeroes who refueled on carriers and then hit Pearl Harbor.

The coffin, corpse, sword, and jewels in the coffin were sent to the National Museum in Taipei, ostensibly for repatriation to Japan—except for one small piece of the coffin. The farmers had broke off a ceramic handle with a tool, and I still have it to this day.

I don't think my fellow security police officers were seeing things! Somehow, I think the two incidents are connected.

—*William Behling, USAF Security Police, retired*

Photographed: A Ghost!

A fellow trooper, Brett Smith, shared this story with me. Brett's wife, Amy, is a real-estate agent in the Monroe County area.

One of our young troops was unable to pass the Field Training Officer Program, so he was dismissed from the department. While in the program he had purchased a home in the area. After being told that he would not be hired, the trooper found other employment outside of Monroe County. Amy decided to help the probationary trooper sell his home. The young trooper still had some of his furniture items in the home that he would pick up later. Brett, Amy, and their two small sons went to the house, because Amy needed to take photos of the house to post on the Internet. As Brett kept his two sons occupied, Amy took photos of each room.

The digital photos were given to the secretary the next day to upload onto the computer. When Amy called the following day to check on the photos, the secretary said they had turned out fine, but she asked about the woman who was in one of the photos.

Amy said there was no woman in the photos, so the secretary sent the photo in question to Amy in an e-mail. Amy was surprised and *shocked*! Amy showed the photo to Trooper Smith, who was also stunned. No one was living in the house when they stopped by and snapped the pictures. Plus, the only people in the home that day were Amy and her family. Amy got hold of the real-estate agent who had sold the home to the young trooper. The agent was familiar with the family, and knew the current address of the woman who had lived there.

The agent showed the photo to the woman, who immediately identified the female as her mother. The shocker—the woman said her mother had been dead for approximately three years! She added that her mother liked to stand by the front door and look out at the neighbors.

—*Herman Brown, trooper*
Michigan State Police, Monroe, Michigan

five

Karma—Twists of Fate

Karma is a concept in Eastern religions that is related to human action and deed. It is believed that karma causes the entire cycle that Westerners know as "cause and effect." In Western religions, karma is regarded more as simple twists of fate. Regardless of terminology, most police officers acknowledge that something extra that is much bigger than themselves exists in impossible situations.

The Fatal Vortex

It seems like it was only yesterday when I was sent to a house alarm call that could have resulted in fatalities. Most house alarm calls are false alarms—the wind blows open a shutter or a resident accidentally sets off the alarm. So I believe it is only by Divine grace that I am alive today to share this story.

I pull into the driveway at the same time the key holder arrives. The key holder is the person an alarm company calls when a house alarm goes off. In this case, it is the homeowner's thirty-year-old son.

I tell the man to stay by his car until I secure the area. He says, "I know my mother is home and everything's cool, but I don't know what is going on."

I checked the doors, windows, and garage entrance for any possible forced entry. Everything looks secure. I say, "Go ahead and open the garage door," and I remind him to stay by his car while I check the inside of the house.

I enter the dimly lit garage and walk to the door that leads into the house. I knock on the door and announce, "State police!" as I push open the door. At that moment, a white-haired elderly woman steps out of nowhere and slowly points a .20 gauge shotgun directly in my face!

Even though I have turned on the garage light, she doesn't seem to notice I am a uniformed trooper. In my attempt to escape the "fatal vortex" and unholster my weapon, I stumble backward but do not fall. The fatal vortex is that hypothetical space we're taught about in school; that space shaped like a funnel that you never want to be caught in.

I was definitely at the tip of that funnel. I had no safety zone and no spatial advantage.

As I try not to lose my balance, I hear CLICK. The old lady has actually pulled the trigger! Not only does this sound signify my life may instantly be over, but it also means she *means* to shoot!

Somehow I know this woman is the resident and not an intruder. I wonder why I didn't draw my weapon before I stepped into the garage, which is what we are taught to do as a precaution. I am grateful I didn't because I might have shot her if my gun had been in my hand. I yell at her repeatedly, "I'm a police officer! I'm a police officer! *Don't shoot! Look at my uniform! I'm a police officer!*"

The woman's son starts yelling at her, too. Who knows what this woman is thinking? How can she not see my uniform? It takes both of us to convince her I am the police and not there to hurt her. It is a miracle she does not kill me.

After I settled her down, I asked, "What were you thinking? Didn't you hear me knocking at the door? Didn't you hear me say 'state police'? Why didn't you call 911? They would have told you who was knocking! When you press the panic button for the alarm, police are *supposed* to come and help you, *right?*" (According to the alarm company, she had pressed the panic button.)

As I'm scolding her and trying to regain my composure, I open the double-barrel action to make the weapon safe. Out pops a shotgun shell! I can see that shell moving in slow motion...jumping out of the chamber into the air...spiraling...twirling...dancing...and then finally hitting the floor with a THUNK and rolling to its final resting place between my two feet. I didn't have to pick it up to know it was a heavy *unspent* round and that by the grace of God the gun hadn't fired.

It humbled me to realize how close I had come to death. And, to make matters worse, I found out she was the widow of a state trooper. I could have killed a fellow trooper's wife!

I shot the gun outdoors. There was nothing wrong with it! The woman pulled the trigger—I should have been killed.

There are some things that have happened to me in this job that I just haven't talked about. This is one of them. I don't know why I didn't shoot that woman, especially after she pulled the trigger. How did I know she was really a "good guy?" Whatever you want to call it—intuition, a sixth sense, or an angel—I depended on it, and we are both alive.

—Craig W. Johnson, trooper
Michigan State Police, West Branch, Michigan

Me: An Unwitting Instrument?

The spring of 1966 was a time of change in my life. I was a sergeant in the patrol division of the Amarillo, Texas, police department. I was supervising a nine man (and three canine) Tactical Unit charged with interrupting felonies in progress—mostly business burglaries and armed robberies. It was my sixth year of service in police work and my thirteenth year as a weekend warrior in the 9th Special Forces Group, United States Army Reserve. I loved both of those jobs.

At age fifteen, I had dropped out of school during my parents' nasty divorce. After years of living with my feelings of inferiority and inadequate preparation, police work and the military had provided opportunities for me to advance in knowledge and status. Among other good things, my long-dormant spiritual life and my religious interest renewed after meeting with members of the Baha'i faith. I began studying the Baha'i writings.

On the other hand, I was also dragged down by depression. I had a wife and a young son, and my marriage of some ten years had fallen apart. We were separated, and I had moved into a tiny, dingy, $10 a week apartment in the back of someone's one-car garage. A brother officer, who I had trained under and greatly admired, was brutally murdered while trying to make a routine arrest on a wild New Year's Eve night.

Paul Arrandondo, who shot my friend in the head in front of thirty witnesses, was found guilty of capital murder in a jury trial. Under Texas legal procedure, the jury sets the penalty, and he was sentenced to ten years in prison. I felt this as a deep insult and an inadequate consequence. Then, not six months later, another officer friend of mine was shot to death while trying to stop a driver in a stolen pickup truck. I brooded about all this and felt survivor's guilt.

Then, with my college graduation ceremony scheduled for the very next day, I got a late night call that my fifty-six-year-old father was en route to a hospital with a possible heart attack. I rushed to the emergency room, arriving just in time to see him gasp his last breath. I missed that graduation, which was important to me.

Thus, my depression worsened. I felt tremendous guilt and believed my wrecked marriage was due to my misbehavior. Police did not go to shrinks in those days. They probably still don't. Back then, if the police brass even suspected that an officer had some mental problem, it was the end of his career.

One night I was especially depressed. I had the night off and was sitting in my dingy little room, taking my personal inventory. I decided that the only sensible thing to do was to kill myself. I knew the cop way to do it right was with a handgun. The business end of the barrel should be against the roof of my mouth. It would all be over in a second. I did not feel afraid. I was too weary for that.

I took out my Smith & Wesson .38 police special and paused for a minute to think about whether there was anything else I needed to do. I did not consider a suicide note to be necessary. They seemed so pathetic. I did pause for a moment to think whether there were any loose ends to tie up.

For some reason when I paused, I remembered a discussion that had taken place a few days before among the members of the Bahá'í faith. We had discussed a message that came to us from our National Spiritual Assembly (NSA) in Chicago. A Bahá'í family of modest economic means from Arizona had asked the NSA for help. Their fourteen-year-old son had run away from home. Oklahoma City Police saw him hitchhiking and had picked him up. While he had not committed any crime, they were holding him in protective custody until his family could get him home. Arizona Bahá'ís had been praying for his safe return. Apparently, there was not yet a Bahá'í unit in Oklahoma City and the NSA hoped that a nearby unit could help by checking on the boy. Our group was not close enough to Oklahoma City. All we did was add our short prayer for his return and moved on to other business.

During my housekeeping moment before suicide, I suddenly, vividly, remembered the discussion about the kid. For some reason, I even remembered his name and the family name. That was unusual in itself, because I had no real interest in their problems. I thought, *I need to take care of this—I can kill myself later.*

I was always short of money in those days, but I did have cash in my pocket that night and gas in my Volkswagen Beetle. My thought process was something like this: *What does it matter if I spend a few hours and my cash doing this? I am going to die anyway so I might as well get the damn kid home—no one else is going to do it. I am an experienced cop. All the Oklahoma police want is to get rid of him safely. That can be done with a non-refundable Greyhound bus ticket to Arizona.*

I put my piece in the drawer, got in my car, and drove east on Highway 66 to Oklahoma City. I had never been there nor did I know how far it was, or how to find the police station when I got there. I don't remember what the trip over was like. I was just focused on getting this one last thing done so I could die. I remember talking to the desk sergeant at their police department. We called the bus station and checked on the cost of a ticket. He agreed to have someone take the kid there by patrol car, buy the ticket, and see him off (it seems the kid was happy to go home by now). I gave the sergeant the fare, plus a few dollars for meals en route.

I remember a little about the trip home. I fell in behind a westbound Greyhound (probably not the one he was on) that was driving about 80 mph and drafted my little 36-horse "People's Joy Wagon" back to Amarillo in the wee hours of the morning. Somewhere along the way, my depression lifted a bit and I decided that suicide was not the way to go.

Not long after that episode in my life, I packed all my personal possessions in an army footlocker, put the footlocker in the back seat of the Beetle, and left Amarillo forever. Anyone who lived through the 1960s knows that the interval from 1966 to 1968 was not a good time to try to deal with depression, but things did eventually improve in my life. I gave up my police career so I could attend graduate school. There were no Army Reserve units close to Carbondale, Illinois, so I resigned my officer's commission. I still suffered from depression during those transitions, but I never again considered suicide.

By the 1970s, I had made new friends and found my true love. I was remarried, and I was building a new career as a university professor, teaching criminal justice at the University of Alabama in Tuscaloosa. I also did polygraph examination work on the side to stay in touch with the criminal world. I found happiness.

Today, the additional forty-fours years I've lived by avoiding suicide seem like a blessing. Being alive is good! Retired from teaching now, I am at peace with myself and the world.

However, that episode with the kid from Arizona still puzzles me. Why did I think about the kid when I was looking down the barrel of that .38 revolver? Why did I decide to put my death on hold long enough to help a complete stranger in a faraway city? That was not the type of hands-on helping person I was then (or now). After such a brief discussion of the kid's situation, why did I remember his name? I have never been any good at remembering even names of people I have actually met briefly.

I did become a Bahá'í, and I have drawn my own conclusions. I went to rescue that kid because I was compelled to do so by something I did not understand at the time. I was compelled because of the prayers of people on behalf of that child. God answered their prayers and I happened to be the instrument used to get the job done. But, what about the other side of the coin? The rescue did save my life. Someone closer to Oklahoma City could have been compelled to help the child. In that case, I likely would have gone through with the suicide. I believe there was some sort of intervention for me.

I firmly believe in the power of prayer. I believe that God answers prayers often by means that unbelievers can easily perceive as coincidental. What do you believe?

—*Vergil Lewis Williams, sergeant, retired*
Amarillo City Police, Amarillo, Texas

The Apple Tree

One Halloween night, some kids cut down a beautiful apple tree in Justice Beeck's backyard as a prank. I was stationed in St. Ignace, Michigan, at the time. A shop teacher, on his way to work, noticed the downed tree and cut a large branch off to take to school. He decided to make a gavel for the judge. He thought it would serve as a lovely token of sympathy for the disheartened judge.

Fortunately, the kids who committed the dastardly deed were apprehended several weeks later. They came up before the judge himself. Ironically, he used his apple tree gavel to administer justice—or should I say "karmic justice"?

—*Donald Hinds, trooper, retired*
Michigan State Police, Norway, Michigan

The Tooth Fairy in Reverse

One afternoon I was called to the scene of a pedestrian vehicle accident at State and Main Streets in Scottville, Michigan. Seven-year-old Christina was crossing the street when she was struck by a man driving a pickup truck. The truck hit her straight-on. She was thrown off her feet before landing on her chin on the concrete. Luckily, Christina had young, supple bones and escaped with minor injuries. Unfortunately, she lost her front tooth. And it was a new permanent tooth.

Emergency medical service arrived and took her to the hospital, while at least ten police and rescue workers remained to look for the little girl's tooth. Adding to the challenge of finding Christina's tooth on the street was that just prior to the incident, a truck had spilled corn from its dump box while rounding the corner. There were THOUSANDS of corn kernels on the street.

We searched for at least forty-five minutes with no luck. Cars drove over the corn, smashing the kernels and turning them into more bits of yellow and white. Finally, we had to give up finding the tooth as an impossible feat. What were the odds of finding a tooth in this mess?

After the last rescue unit pulled away, I drove to my office to finish writing the accident report. As I was sitting at my desk, the hospital phoned. I talked to a doctor and he pleaded, "Would you just look one more time for the tooth?"

Although another thirty minutes had gone by, I complied with his request. I truly imagined the tooth was stuck in some car's tire by now,. But for some reason, I still saw *possibility*. Looking for a tooth among thousands of kernels of corn was more frustrating than looking for a needle in a haystack.

I finally said to myself, *"Okay ... enough of this ... the tooth is still here, it has to be. But, where did it go?"* All of a sudden the answer came to me clearly—backtrack the incident again. All right, she was hit right here, which caused her to be knocked forward about here ... I carefully paced out the area and totally guessed where Christina had landed and hit her chin. Then, I see something in the corn that didn't look quite right. The color blended in perfectly, but something about it caught my eye. I bent down to get a closer look. Could it be? Yes! It wasn't corn. It was her tooth!

I was so excited for Christina that I hopped into my patrol car and drove to a Shell Mini Mart, grabbed a pint of milk out of the cooler, and dropped the tooth into the milk. My wife, who is a dental assistant, said that is the first thing you do to save a tooth. I yelled to the cashier as I ran out the door, "I'll be back to pay for this later!" Fortunately, she knew me. I raced to the hospital with lights flashing and siren blaring, and ran into the emergency room with the tooth.

The doctor implanted the tooth—and it survived! All I could think of was what a *blessing* to find it! I swear, it was like looking for one bean in a silo of beans—it seemed impossible. Several of us had already looked at that spot and couldn't see it. But, when I stopped, tuned in, and didn't try so hard, the tooth was suddenly *there*—in full view.

Christina visits each year, to show me her tooth and her smile. She thanks me every time she sees me. And, yes, I did go back and pay for the milk.

—*Larry D. Nichols, chief of police*
Scottville Police Department, Scottville, Michigan

Fore!

It was a cold, cloudy Saturday in late January of 1975. Several other troopers and I were working a day shift at the state police post in Flint, Michigan. I had patrolled north on the I-75 freeway, wrote a couple of tickets, served a subpoena for a court case scheduled for early the next week, and checked out a rest area known for illicit activity.

Usually, the Flint Post area provided any and all kinds of criminal activity and a variety of traffic offenses because of the three nearby expressways. We were usually "huntin' and confrontin'!" But it was an unusually mild day and mid morning when another trooper radioed my unit.

"14, you ready for one?"

"Name it, 10."

"How 'bout Petko on Miller?"

"Sounds good. I'll meet you there." I called the post as I entered the restaurant parking lot: 35–14 to 35."

"Go ahead, 14" came the response from the desk sergeant.

"I'll be out with 10 at Petko on Miller."

"It's your daily," came the terse reply. This was the sergeant's reference to our daily reports that wouldn't reflect any activity other than a coffee break for the next fifteen minutes or so. It wasn't really busy yet, and we'd easily catch up after a cup, or three.

"Crime will have to wait a few minutes, " I responded. Little did I know how short those few minutes would become.

"Clear on it, KQA 273" the sergeant said.

Petko was known for good coffee and good food, as well as lovely and attentive waitresses. They were witty, sometimes flirtatious, and they liked a law enforcement presence in the restaurant. We were lucky. Two of our favorite waitresses took our order. After some back-and-forth banter and laughs, we sipped our first cup of coffee. Everyone was enjoying the brief interlude until my coffee partner was told the post desk sergeant wanted to speak with either him or me on the restaurant's phone. The other trooper, one year senior to me in the department, took the call.

He came back to the table, chugged the remaining coffee in his cup, and said to me and the two waitresses, "It's been a great party, and we wish we didn't have to drink and run, but a body has been found on the side of I-69, just west of Swartz Creek. Leave some money Charlie, and follow me." I gave the girls a couple of dollar bills and tried to catch Harry, who was screaming out of the parking lot.

It was red lights and sirens for the five miles we had to travel west on the I-69 freeway west of Flint. A Swartz Creek patrol car was parked on the south side of I-69, having responded to the Genesee County Central Dispatch request for units to respond to the scene. It looked like we'd be backing up the Swartz Creek Police Department and assisting their officer with the investigation. We parked our hot patrol cars behind the Swartz Creek car and approached the officer, who was kneeling over a prone male's body on the shoulder of the freeway. This young officer, who we both knew and worked with, greeted us with the news.

"The kid's dead and the scene is outside our jurisdiction. What would you guys like me to do?" He backed away from the body.

Harry and I looked at the body and observed bloody matted hair on the back of his head. Harry checked for a pulse in the subject's neck area and found none. Harry looked up from his kneeling position.

"Charlie, radio the post, not Central Dispatch, and ask for some detectives. Request that the crime lab in Bridgeport be notified. Terry (Swartz Creek police officer) can help protect the scene and keep any gawkers moving in both directions!"

I radioed the post at Harry's request. The sergeant advised he'd notify some post detectives, the crime lab, and post and district supervisors. As I was replacing the microphone on the dashboard of the car, Harry came up with the victim's Michigan driver's license. I put it on my clipboard, which was on the front seat of the patrol car. I noticed that the victim was eighteen years old and lived in Flint.

While awaiting further information and direction from the post, we checked around the body and found nothing that looked significant. A detective who happened to live near Swartz Creek drove up and parked. We briefed him on our findings and I gave him the victims ID. Soon the Genesee County medical examiner arrived and pronounced the victim deceased. We could have told him that.

An ambulance crew from Flint arrived. At the detectives direction, the crew moved, then loaded the body into the ambulance. When the body was removed, we could all observe small pieces of yellow thread lying on the ground amongst some small insects and spiders that had been on the victims clothing.

The detective on the crime scene kept in contact with the post and the other detective who was called in to work on the investigation. After a while, the crime-scene detective advised us that the other detective had contacted the victim's mother and learned from her the names of two friends her son had left the house with the night before. Her son and two friends were going out Friday night and both friends were identified to the follow-up detective.

The victim's friend was contacted and brought into the Flint Post for an interview. During the conversation, this subject advised the detective that he had picked up the victim and another friend. The three of them got some beer and were riding around some back roads west of Flint, drinking. After a while, an argument ensued between the victim, who was sitting in the front passenger seat of the car, and the buddy who was in the right rear seat of the car. The argument became very heated and the driver stated to the detective that the back seat passenger pulled out a gun and shot the front seat passenger in the back of the head.

The driver stated they all realized their friend was badly wounded and panicked. They had stopped the car along I-69 to dump the victim's body. The driver stated that the shooter was the only one who got out to pull the victim from the car. The driver and the shooter drove to Flint and went to their respective homes.

During the interview, the driver insisted he only drove the car and did not help the shooter remove the victim's body from the car. The driver told the detective who the shooter was, and gave permission to search his room and car for any other evidence.

Nothing of evidentiary value was found in the driver's house, but in checking the subject's car, the detective noticed some blood stains in the passenger's front seat area and cheap yellow shag carpeting throughout the car's interior. After consulting via radio with the on-scene detective, the yellow threads found at the scene sounded as if they were similar to what was noted in the car. The car was then seized and the driver detained and kept locked up at the Flint Post.

A trooper helped the detective locate the suspected shooter at his home. He willingly agreed to go with them to the post and give a statement. After some hedging and realizing the driver had given him up as the shooter, the suspect confessed and agreed to tell his version of the story.

There was word from the Bridgeport Post that the crime lab personnel were en route to our location, but that they didn't know when they would arrive. We walked around the scene, looking for any evidence while awaiting their arrival. We found nothing but used golf balls. The Genesee Valley Golf Course was located on the north side of I-69, directly opposite our crime scene. Errant tee shots had apparently found their way across four lanes of traffic and a wide median to land near where we were searching. I quickly pocketed some of the better balls found in hopes of using them on area courses during the coming spring. It was like an Easter egg hunt, with shiny new balls everywhere. *What a bonanza*, I thought!

While awaiting the arrival of the crime lab, word came from the post detective that the shooter implicated the driver as helping to get rid of the gun used in the shooting. The shooter advised he used a .38 special six-shot revolver and gave it to the driver after "they" dragged the victim from the car. The shooter said the driver, while driving quickly eastbound from the scene, rolled down his window and threw the gun with his left hand over the top of the car. The shooter stated that there should be five live rounds in the chamber. The detective advised to start walking through the dead weeds to try and locate the murder weapon. After twenty minutes of futile searching, I told Harry to meet me back at the crime scene. I pulled up my patrol car, rolled down the window, and told Harry to follow me on foot.

As I drove rapidly eastbound on the shoulder of I-69, I threw the found golf balls over the top of the patrol car with my left hand, one after another. Harry watched where they landed, and after the fourth ball was thrown, he told me to turn around and return to the starting point. He proudly and carefully lifted a shiny blue revolver by the trigger guard as I pulled to a stop near him. The gun was in his right hand, and a Wilson Staff golf ball was in his left! Hallelujah! Who needed the crime lab?

After further investigation, background work, lab analysis, and reinterviewing two suspects, open murder charges were issued. My first homicide crime scene turned out to be successful in that justice for the young victim was served. Lengthy sentences were handed down by the Genesee County Circuit Court. Both subjects confessed and told similar stories. The driver received the same sentence as the shooter once everything finally came out. Finding the gun with the driver's fingerprints on it led to a decisive plea bargain.

All of us involved felt sad for the young victim who had died because of an argument over whether to get more beer or to go home. Bad, alcohol-fueled logic was used. Tragically, what should have been an easy day of work turned into a creative, team effort to give justice to the victim and his family.

Thank God for errant tee shots!

—Charles D. Gross, detective sergeant, retired
Michigan State Police, Marquette, Michigan

Karmic Happenings

Early one evening, I was patrolling alone and decided to stop a vehicle with its taillight out. As I walked up to the car, the male driver jumped out. He was noticeably upset.

"Please, officer. Don't arrest me! I'm suspended," he begged. "In fact, I'm *very suspended*. I don't have a license. I know there is a warrant out for me ... *please* don't arrest me." He was actually shaking. I genuinely felt sorry for him, but cautiously directed him to return to his car.

I said, "Calm down. No matter what happens, everything will be okay. Be seated in your car and let me run your name through the computer. Let me see what is going on for you."

He would not stop pleading. He said, "I have this date. I have a date with a woman tonight—the first date I've had in years. I know *she's the one*! If you arrest me today, she'll never go out with me!"

I thought to myself, *If he is making up this story, then he is one fabulous liar because his tears, disposition, and behavior seem incredibly real and indicative of a truthful person.* When I ran his name through the computer, he was *very* suspended all right. He had been arrested on two different occasions for driving while suspended and he had many points on his license dating back several years. Apparently, he was suspended because of his poor driving. In this case, however, I hadn't stopped him for a driving violation, merely having a taillight out. I walked back to the car.

His voice cracked as he spoke. "This this w-woman, is my s-soul mate. I-I know she is ..." he sniffled. "I've b-been looking for her for l-lifetimes! I-I know you don't believe me, but if you arrest me, we will n-never marry l-like we're s-supposed to. If you arrest me, it'll n-never happen! I've been so lonely, and, finally, I f-found her." He went on and on, crying, but I believed him. This wasn't an act.

In my department, patrolmen have discretion and are empowered to make decisions—whether to write a citation, for example, and ask the person to appear in court later, or to physically lodge a person in jail. What made my job difficult sometimes was that as a female officer, I was often harshly judged by my male peers and accused of being too soft.

This man's arrest would have looked great on my statistics, but I felt it would unnecessarily screw up the man's life. He was respectful and honest with me, so I chose to let him go. I listened to my heart.

I wrote him a citation for driving while suspended and told him to walk across the street to the gas station and call a taxi. I warned him he was not allowed to drive and then I left.

I am sure he probably drove off in his car, but I didn't care. He hadn't committed any traffic violation and I knew he would show up in court. It was going to cost him several hundred dollars in fines to take care of the matter and he'd probably lose another year of driving privileges. I thought nothing more about the matter and by the next day I had completely forgotten the incident.

Two years later, I was still a patrolman, and I was feeling down and out because I'd been passed by several times for promotion, most likely because I was a softy. When I stopped people on patrol, I tried to be fair. When I was dispatched to crime scenes, even the most non-serious in nature, I treated people with care and dignity the way I would want to be treated. In many cases, I could have said, "I'm sorry, I can't help you. This is not a police matter," or "I'm sorry, this is a civil matter, you'll have to go to small claims court," or "There were no laws broken and I have ten other calls I must go to today"—but I didn't. I helped everyone I could, even if it really wasn't my job. I was beginning to believe my department penalized me for this behavior, for being a true public servant, so I was disgruntled.

One night, I stopped yet another vehicle with a taillight out. This time, however, when the driver jumped out of his car, I could tell he was angry and ready for combat. Plus, he smelled strongly of intoxicants. He was obviously drunk, with bloodshot eyes and slurred speech. He could barely stand up. I knew instantly I was about to get into a fight.

I said, "Sir, please get back in your car." It appeared like he wanted to run. I said, "Okay, sir. You are now under arrest," and the fight was on!

Because it wasn't dark yet, I did not have a partner with me. As I tried to put handcuffs on the man, I was asking for backup on my radio prep. Central Dispatch could hear the man screaming in the background and calling me every dirty name in the book. Although I was in the best shape I had ever been, I am only five feet, two inches tall and I weighed 128 pounds. This man was big. He had to be five ten and at least 250 pounds. I thought, *I'm totally screwed!* I didn't think I had a chance of avoiding injury.

He resisted when I tried to put the cuffs on him; soon we were tumbling in the snow bank. As we wrestled, I thought maybe the snow and cold weather would affect his agility, but he just seemed to get stronger and stronger! He took several swings toward my face, which I managed to avoid. I was now eating quite a bit of snow and my hands were numb. It definitely seemed like I was going to get the worst of it.

As I continued rolling and doing somersaults in the snow with this man, I noticed the headlights of a semi-truck pull in and park behind my patrol car. The truck driver, who was fortunately a good-sized man himself, ran to my rescue. It was a bit humbling to me, but I was grateful he came to my aid. He towered over the drunk, lifted him by his collar, and said, "This little lady said you're under arrest. You're under arrest!" The truck driver tossed the drunk in the backseat of the patrol car like a toy. Somehow during the havoc I had managed to cuff the guy. I slammed the patrol car door and said, "If you break *anything* in my patrol car, I'll submit for a warrant for destroying police property. *That's a five-year felony!*" I was peeved.

As I shook the snow off my pants, I sheepishly looked at the truck driver and said, "Thank you. That was very nice of you to stop and help me. I am truly grateful."

He looked at me and said, "We got married!" I looked at him blankly. "You don't recognize me, do you?" He grinned.

I surveyed his face and said, "No, I'm afraid not, though you do look a little familiar." I always say this to people when they recognize me but I don't recognize them. It softens the blow to the other person, but I had absolutely no idea who this man was or where I might have seen him before.

He said, "I am the man you stopped two years ago, my car had a taillight out."

I wondered, *Does this man realize how many cars I've stopped in the course of two years? Geez!* I politely said, "Gosh, I can't remember, sir, who you are. I'm sorry."

"You stopped me on M-72. Remember? I had a suspended license, and when I told you I had a date with my soul mate, you decided not to take me to jail." Then I remembered.

"Why, of course," I said, "you're the man who was so upset about losing his lady friend. Yes, I remember now!"

The truck driver added, "I recognized you instantly, even though I couldn't see your face, as you were rolling in the snow bank…I knew it was my turn to help you now!"

I hoped he didn't see my face turn red. Like most people, he recognized me from behind. I have an unusual, pear-shaped body. I tried to hide my embarrassment with another "Thank you."

Then, he added, "And I want you to know, I got my license back, went to truck driving school, and we did end up getting married! You made a real difference in my life."

Now, my heart melted, and in that moment, I started to feel better about the work I do.

The man said, "I believe in karma ... I believe it was all supposed to happen this way."

I thought, *What goes around, comes around—what a strange, but fortunate, series of coincidences!* Although, maybe it really was karma.

> —Ingrid P. Dean, detective sergeant, retired
> Michigan State Police, Traverse City, Michigan

How Could this Possibly Happen?

Several years ago, when I was on patrol, I received a call for police assistance regarding a car/motorcycle crash. My partner and I responded to the location. When we arrived, we found a male subject lying face down in the ditch. It was the motorcyclist, and he was pronounced dead at the scene. We noticed the car with heavy damage to the passenger side door. The motorcyclist had come over a hill just as the car pulled into a driveway from the road. The motorcyclist was speeding. The driver of the car had no time to avoid the collision, and the motorcyclist hit the side of the car at full speed.

The driver was white as a ghost and appeared to be in total shock. Shock is not rare in such a situation, but this man appeared to be in a trance. He stared blankly as he recalled what had happened.

He explained, "I'm from over 150 miles away from here. I drove north to meet my friend at this house. I was just pulling into his driveway when the motorcycle hit me. We were planning a fishing trip to Canada. I haven't been here in a long time ..."

The man was in "the zone" and I wasn't about to interrupt him. I couldn't identify what his stare was all about, though. All I knew was that something was very wrong. It was as if he'd had his own near-death experience.

"When the motorcycle hit my car, I saw the man's body fly into the ditch. There wasn't anything I could have done to avoid it." He was shaking his head slowly as he spoke, as if I wasn't there. "I get out of my car, but suddenly I see my sister-in-law running down the road. She is screaming and running to the man in the ditch ... my SISTER-IN-LAW!" The man hesitated.

"Officer, I thought it was a dream ... I thought, how can this possibly be? My sister-in-law, she lives downstate, over a two-hour drive from here. I thought I was seeing a ghost. Then, it all suddenly dawned on me ..." The man's voice trembled and trailed off in silence, as I tried to comprehend what he is saying. He sadly utters, "That was my brother on the motorcycle."

I said, "What?"

He continued, "I knew we each had a friend in this area, but we never knew each other's friends personally. We had no idea we'd both be here today. I haven't even seen my brother in quite some time, because we live so far apart from each other. I can't believe we're in this same town together! How could I be here just in time for him to hit me?"

I stood there, astonished, feeling great sadness for the man. As we sorted things out, I learned his brother was helping a friend repair his motorcycle. He was simply test riding his friend's motorcycle when the accident occurred. Neither brother knew they would see each other.

What were the odds that a man kills his own brother in an accident so far away from both of their homes?

What were the odds that this could happen?

—Duane H. Leroy, chief of police, retired
Leslie Police Department, Michigan

Aggie

Aggie is my child. I'd forgotten what it was like to be loved unconditionally until this feisty, shaggy, red toy poodle came into my life. Dogs have no sense of time. They live moment to moment. When I come home from work, no matter how tough my day, Aggie greets me like a long-lost lover and licks all my woes away!

At only twelve weeks old, she jumped into the hot tub to be with me (of course, not realizing there was water in this strange contraption). She was full of life. She smelled every new smell, heard every new sound, and had to touch everything that crossed her path. She was, and still is, so innocent.

A husband and wife brought an American pit bull terrier into the state police post one day. It had been running around the neighborhood, loose, and it appeared exhausted, heat-stricken, and thirsty. None of the uniformed troopers wanted anything to do with that dog and, conveniently, left the post. I took the dog upstairs to my office into the air conditioning, gave it water, and waited patiently for someone from the dog pound to arrive. It had no collar, but I knew that someone owned this beautiful dog.

The dog pound personnel never arrived. I decided to take the dog home with me, just for one night. I alerted all the appropriate parties that I had the dog—in case the owner should call in looking for it. I had raised pit bull terriers long ago. This dog instantly trusted me. It could sit, lie down, and shake hands. It followed my every command.

I kept the dog in my studio, an unattached building next to my house. I had no intent for this dog, or my Aggie, to ever meet. The American pit was just a huge, big baby. We played tug of war with a towel and it loved the attention. Then I went into the house to see Aggie.

Aggie, of course, had to go pee. I put her outside on her dog leash, tied securely to the back deck on the lake side. She loves the outdoors and "yaps" at every squirrel and at every duck that flies by. I thought, *As long as Aggie is tied up, I'll take the pit to go potty as well—only I'll walk him on a leash, away from Aggie.* It wasn't that I didn't trust the pit bull terrier around my dog, but I didn't know how it would react around other animals.

The dog was so big I had to create a leash for her. Using a sturdy, nylon chord, I designed the loop in a choker style that would fit around her muscular neck and tighten as I pulled it. What I didn't realize, however, is that it loosened quickly and didn't have much friction.

When I took her outside, she heard Aggie barking, and her ears suddenly stood up instantly with great interest. She sat down and peered in Aggie's direction. My house was between the two dogs, so the pit bull couldn't see her. When she sat down, however, the noose around her neck slackened, and her head came right out of the noose.

I can still see all of this in slow motion. I was in terrible distress and knew I was in trouble. The dog charged in Aggie's direction, while I helplessly ran after it. Aggie didn't even know what hit her. She never knew what a "mean" dog was. This dog had predatory instincts and was not socially trained.

The pit attacked Aggie like a wild boar. It made all the same sounds of a wild animal that had just hunted down its prey and now it was ready for the kill. It wrapped its jaws around her neck and lifted her like a toy. It shook Aggie like a rag doll while she screamed for her life.

It is difficult to describe all the emotions that flooded into my soul, but inside I started screaming, *Noooooooooooooooo! This can't be happening to me! Aggie is my everything! My best friend! God, please don't take her! I GIVE IN! I can't fix this situation by myself!*

As I wrapped my hands around the pit's gripping jaws— with no regard or sense for what the pit could possibly do to me—I struggled and pried with all my might. Her jaws wouldn't move and her excitement seemed to keep on growing over this new "toy!" In between all my emotions, it seemed like something shifted in me. There was a remembrance that *anything* is possible in life, and that Aggie could live—even in this ominous, impossible situation. There was a moment of total understanding that I couldn't save the dog by myself and that only something very universal and experiential could alter this situation—and I beckoned it. Alone, I couldn't bend 2,400 pounds of jaw pressure.

There was no time to go get my departmental handgun. If I rushed for the gun, both dogs would be dead. Then, the miracle happened...

My home is at the end of a dirt road in a rural area. I live alone and have very few visitors—maybe once per week, at the most. There are two homes, twenty-five to thirty yards away on each side of my house, whose owners are part-time, seasonal residents. Neither of the owners was home. One of the neighbors, however, had hired two male workers to lay patio stone near his porch, and they saw me, struggling in distress.

It should be noted that in the twenty years I had lived at my house, neither of my neighbors have ever had people working on their houses—especially when they were not around.

The two workers, in their mid-twenties or early thirties, both very strong and able, came to my aid and helped me pry the pit's jaws off my dog. As I grabbed my dog and removed the leash from her collar, she laid in my arms, motionless. I was very certain she was dead. It was like holding a child who trusted you, and I ran with her to my back door. As I looked back at the two men, I could see them both laying cock-eyed over the dog, one sitting on the dog, while the other still held its jaws open. The one man yelled, somewhat concerned, "What do we do now?"

I intuitively and spontaneously answered, "Let it go! It likes humans! I think it just doesn't like other animals!"

Interestingly, no sooner than the two men let the dog go, the pit knew exactly where I was standing and that it's trophy was in my arms. It immediately ran, lunged onto my back deck, giving me barely enough time to slam the back door into its face. I remember it standing on its back legs with its front paws on the glass door, wagging its tail. Then it sat down and stared at me intently, as if asking, "Aren't you going to let me in? Why won't you let me in?"

Now was not the time to try sorting out how I felt, especially with a dead dog in my hands and blood everywhere. I laid Aggie down on the floor and she suddenly woke up! She wasn't dead! She was in shock, but barking fiercely as if trying to just get the last word in.

I rushed to the phone and called a fellow trooper at the state police post. The trooper called the veterinarian for me, alerting the doctor that a toy poodle was being rushed to their emergency facility and that the dog might need surgery. I secured the pit bull inside my studio again, and then rushed my dog for immediate care.

Aggie stayed overnight at the vet and it was fortunate she did not need surgery. She had some serious puncture wounds on her neck, which never pierced through the artery. She was extremely lucky to have survived. She made a full recovery, with no post-traumatic issues.

The pit bull was lucky to have survived, too. She spent the night in my studio while Aggie was in the hospital, and then an animal control officer picked her up. I felt bad, actually, that I couldn't find its owner. I called animal control for two days, and she still hadn't been picked up. The animal control officer said the dog would probably be euthanized.

One might wonder why this upset me so much, since the pit had nearly killed my best friend and couldn't be trusted around other animals—but the thought of the dog being euthanized mortified me. I hoped for another miracle—that the owner would be found. I wanted one last shot at scolding and reprimanding this individual. Then, another miracle happened.

The animal control officer called and said the owner had claimed the dog. It was a young *woman* owner! I thought to myself, *no wonder the dog liked me and did tricks for me. Its owner is female, like me.*

I visited the young woman and told her what happened. I scolded her. She explained that the dog had gotten off its leash and ran off without her knowing for some time that it was gone. She knew the pit bull didn't like other animals but that she loved people. She had adopted the dog and simply didn't know how to train it.

I told her to take it to a professional trainer, and that pit bull terriers (especially pure breeds) are very intelligent. It was young enough to be socialized. I told her that the dog was not the responsible party regarding this mishap—that, as its owner, she was the one responsible. I didn't give her the vet bill, because from where she lived, it looked like she didn't have extra money to spend.

I don't believe guns kill people, either, but rather that people do. If we own a dog, a gun, or any potentially dangerous piece of property—people have to be held responsible. Banning guns or banning dogs is not the solution.

—*Amy Anderson, detective sergeant*
Michigan State Police

six
The Police Heart

Emotional intelligence as a quality of the infinite Self goes far beyond our ego; it goes beyond Freud's superego of conditioning and habituation. It is not just a counterbalance or an opposite of our IQ. It is powerful. The integration of both the rational and the intuitive comprises the full extent of our aptitude. Some people have a high degree of intelligence in both areas, while others have little of either. I believe police officers in particular have high potential to develop both areas of intelligence, because they are forced to use both their rational and emotional mind to stay alive. They also develop an unusual humor in order to cope with the trauma they experience.

Police officers see and experience emotions so powerful that they are rarely shared with the public. May readers better understand why police officers keep these emotions to themselves. Do not read this chapter if you are unwilling to experience the gifts of emotion on a more spiritual, influential level.

Humorous stories are strategically placed to help readers recover emotionally from the more powerful stories in this chapter. Humor is what helps officers restore and refuel for the emotional challenges in their jobs.

The Little Boy

I was the first police officer at the scene of a one-car accident, arriving only minutes after it happened. It was the middle of the night and, except for my red patrol lights going round and round, the road was dark and lonely. Whoever had called in this accident was nowhere to be seen.

A woman had rolled her SUV and was smashed between the driver's seat and steering wheel. She was dead. The silence gave a false sense of peace—until I heard the whimpering of a child. I walked around the vehicle, which was lying on its side, and saw a little boy lying underneath it. The roof covered and pinned half his body, while his head and arms were free. I was alarmed.

There was no way I could lift that vehicle! I phoned to make sure help was coming. I prayed that just one car with a bunch of people in it would drive by. But nobody came.

The child was conscious and in a surprised voice asked, "Are you a *real* state trooper?"

I chuckled, "Of course I am, silly! I know you asked because I'm just a girl, huh?"

The boy gave a half-smile and then blurted out, "I want my mom! Where is my mom?" Suddenly, marble-sized tears fell down his cheeks. I saw no reason to tell him that his mother had died. Instead, I tried to reassure him.

"My friends are helping her. They're going to take her to the hospital. But, you know what? I don't have any children. Could I be like your mom just for a while?"

He nodded his head and said, "Okay ..." I took his hand in mine.

He was a sweet-faced boy with brown, curly locks. He had the most beautiful big eyes I'd ever seen. He looked up at me seriously. "Am I going to die?" he asked.

For a split second, I choked. He had obvious internal bleeding; things didn't look too good. I regained my composure and without hesitation said, "No, you won't die. You know, whether you decide to live in heaven, or if you choose to stay right here on earth, either way ... you will still be you, and you will still be alive. Nobody ever dies. We all live forever."

He looked into my eyes and I felt that he understood.

With the hint of a smile, he squeezed my hand in trust. After what seemed like an eternal moment, he took his last breath and gently passed away.

—*Ingrid P. Dean, detective sergeant, retired*
Michigan State Police, Traverse City, Michigan

What Child Is This?

It was the middle of the night. The bars had just closed when I arrived at the scene of a single-car accident. A car had hit a telephone pole with such impact that the telephone pole was completely obliterated and was lying horizontally on the ground. The car was resting on its roof.

The lights from my patrol car intermittently shined on the vehicle, and I could hear emergency vehicle sirens on their way. The female driver had been thrown from the vehicle. I could smell intoxicants on her breath as she lay motionless—actually sleeping—on the ground nearby. I attempted to talk with her, but she was so drunk that she didn't even know she had been in an accident.

As the ambulance neared, I looked at the mangled vehicle, thinking how lucky the woman was to be alive. I don't know what it was, but something drew my eyes to the vehicle's interior, just as the patrol car lights lit up the scene like a strobe. I saw a little boy—standing erect inside the car, his feet firmly planted on the upside-down roof! Amazed, I blinked my eyes to focus.

He was about three feet tall and probably four years old. Each time the strobe-like light shined on the car, I saw him. I ran to the car and searched for an opening large enough that I could reach him with my arms. He was in shock and didn't seem to know I was there. He just stood straight up, like a soldier at attention. He was sniffling and quietly moaning, as if he had been taught not to cry. His left arm looked broken and limp as he held it.

I reached through a crumpled window and carefully lifted the boy. Wonderingly, I took him out of the vehicle and cradled him in my arms, as though he were my own son. I gave him a teddy bear that I carry in the patrol car and said, "There now, everything will be all right." He clutched the stuffed animal with his right arm, as though he would never let it go.

After inspecting the scene, I couldn't figure out where the boy had come from. How had he survived the accident? The car was hardly recognizable. How could I have missed him inside that mangled mess? There was no blood on him. Had he been thrown from the vehicle and then walked back in? Or had he been in a seat and then extricated himself?

There is nothing terribly more significant about this incident, except that I will never forget the vision of him standing inside that car, alone, hurt, and confused.

—*John G. Arthur, trooper*
Michigan State Police, Traverse City, Michigan

Love Train
Excerpt from the book
Alaska Behind Blue Eyes by Alan L. White

Skagway, Alaska, a town with little more than 850 residents, is nestled within an impressive array of mountains that claw at the sky. These rugged peaks create a nearly impassible barrier to the Canadian interior.

Today, in early spring, when lawns have turned green and lower elevation trees explode with new life, the old steam engine is brought out of storage for the season's first run through White Pass over a narrow-gauge track that was installed in 1897. This is always a highly publicized event, with many local residents riding the inaugural trip over the pass.

Old Number 73 has left the station and begun its long journey toward White Pass.

I am working the 4:00 PM to midnight shift, fighting a bout of cynicism and generally feeling sorry for myself. All the problems associated with being twenty-something surge through my head. Even in the land of my dreams, Alaska, the thought of life passing me by is overpowering. As I drive up to the railroad shops on Skagway's north end, I am in no mood for the strange vehicle that is parked beyond the cluttered buildings.

The car sits alongside the tracks, far beyond the rail yards and near the Gold Rush Cemetery. From a distance, I can see two people in the front seat. The car is an old Chevy Nova that, apparently, has been driven on a lot of bad roads. A battered Yukon license plate hangs awkwardly from the rear bumper.

Suddenly angry, I drive toward the car grudgingly, feeling obligated to investigate the suspicious intruder. As I slowly pull up behind the car, Old Number 73 is picking up speed. In my present mood, I am already furious with the vehicle's occupants for forcing me to provide police service. I park at the rear bumper and angrily exit my unit.

A poorly dressed middle-aged man steps from the car and meets me halfway. He seems to be somewhat embarrassed. "Am I doing something wrong, officer?" he asks, avoiding eye contact while looking down the tracks.

"Let's see some identification," I scowl.

"Yes, ah, sure, officer. Anything you want." He pulls out a battered leather wallet from his pocket and removes a Yukon driver's license.

"Canyon?" I say, surprised he has traveled so far in this wreck of a car.

"Yes, sir. I was able to get my shift at the mine covered. We headed out this morning," he replied, still looking for the oncoming train.

"So ... what brings you to Skagway?" I sarcastically ask, more annoyed now than suspicious.

"My son likes to see the train. It's kind of special for him. He's been waiting all winter for the first run." I look beyond the Nova and can see black smoke from Old Number 73 slowly making its way up the tracks. *At least the train will pass soon and they'll leave*, I think, wishing the locomotive would hurry. They weren't doing anything wrong, minor trespassing perhaps, but nothing serious. I just wanted them gone and out of my hair.

Forcing myself to continue the investigation, I bend over and look inside the car at the guy's son, expecting to see a young boy.

He must have been about my age. A birth defect has caused weak neck muscles that are unable to support his head, and it flops from side to side. But he is looking down the tracks. Skinny arms with uncontrollable, twisted hands swat at nothing. A long string of drool drains from his mouth to a large wet spot on his collarless shirt. A battered wheelchair lays in the backseat, folded, to complete this depressing collage.

"Train, Daddy! Train, Daddy!" he spits out with glee. The train is indeed approaching as I stand quietly with absolutely nothing to say.

"We drive down each year for the first run of the season," the man says, looking at the approaching smoke. "My son likes trains. He likes the rumble they make."

I think, *Please stop talking. I have heard enough.*

"We left early this morning. The trip takes a long time because we have to stop a lot."

Please, just shut up. I don't want to hear anymore, I scream to myself.

"It sure does make him happy. Whenever he sees a train on TV or in a book, he smiles. This one's his favorite though."

Inside I struggle for something to say, but words won't come. Five minutes ago I was filled with anger—and now, three hundred seconds later, I am awash in emotions I hardly understand. "Train, Daddy! Train!" his son squeals, his hands flailing up and down.

Old Number 73 roars by us like black thunder, the rail bed shakes under its heavy antique power. The boy laughs and screeches as his father walks around to be near him at the passenger door. I watch father and son share a moment of simple joy. A joy I took for granted, at least until today.

He is not a man of money, of that I am certain. The day off work is no doubt one without pay and will surely affect his monthly bills. But, he loves his son so much he has sacrificed this day to please him. I feel sick inside. *How could I be so self-involved?* My mind swims with various Bible passages I'd learned in my youth, each fitting this scene like a glove.

Self-sacrifice and undying love—a lesson is being learned, right here, right now. I can feel it inside me.

I watch the pair as the train passes and finally disappears around the curve. Choking back tears, I walk toward them. Still excited, his son is trying to call back the train. They face a six-hour drive after this brief moment of joy, and I have a sudden urge to do something. I owe it to them for my self-righteousness, but am having trouble keeping my composure.

"Old Number 73 will be back in about an hour. You get to see it again before we go home," the man says, smiling down at his son, who claps and squeals as he squirms around in the seat. I am pacing in a circle. I want to leave. This is not a comfortable situation for me. *That was it! I was not comfortable! My God*, I thought, *what have I become?*

"Sir, once the train is back at the station, it will make another run tonight. Would you and your son like to ride up the pass?" I ask, determined to make up for my internal cynicism.

The man frowns and walks away quickly from the car. He lowers his voice, so his son cannot hear.

"I checked on the tickets officer. They're very expensive. I only have enough gas money to get home," he says, looking at the dusty ground.

"Don't worry, sir," I reply as I wipe the corner of one eye. "The conductor owes me a favor. I'll get you both on for free."

"You sure officer? You don't have to do that." He is staring much too directly into my eyes.

"Yes, I do, sir," I say, hoping he will not ask me any more questions. "You wait here with your son and watch the train return, and then meet me at the train station. I'll take care of everything."

"My son will like that a lot," he says, looking away.

"I know he will." I turn to leave while I can still talk. I drive to the railroad office and find a parking space among the many vehicles in the lot. I had lied about the conductor owing me a favor—I purchase two passes for the next ride.

Tourists are pouring out of the parlor cars when the father and son arrive at the station. It is not easy to get his son loaded in the observation seat, but we manage. Standing back on the outside step, I watch these two people become so excited for what others take for granted. I love the way I feel inside. My own concerns are fading away and becoming insignificant.

Minutes later, the engine belches black smoke and the whistle blows its evening song.

Before leaving the station, I purchase some train souvenirs and pick up a brochure displaying Old Number 73. The man had locked his car, but my slim-jim tool quickly takes care of that obstacle. After I place the items on the front seat and re-lock the car door, I return to patrolling—with an inner peace I hadn't felt in a long time.

—*Alan White, patrol officer*
Clare Police Department, Clare, Michigan

Fresh Meat

One quiet summer night, about 2:00 AM, my partner and I were driving in the middle of nowhere. There wasn't a soul in sight. As I drove near a familiar state game area, I decided to park the patrol car by an old covered-bridge that crossed over a small stream. The bridge was actually closed for safety reasons, but we could get out and stretch our legs.

I pulled the car to the side of the dirt road about halfway into the brush, and my partner and I got out to enjoy the fresh air and to take a break from driving in unproductive circles. We had been talking for a few minutes when a car came down the roadway toward the bridge. Two couples got out; we could hear their conversation clearly.

One couple decided to walk down the road a bit while the other couple stayed on the bridge. They would each have some time alone with their dates. The two couples agreed to meet back at the car in about forty-five minutes. My partner and I were standing about twenty-five feet from the couple on the bridge, but it was incredibly dark, and they had no idea that two male troopers were nearby.

We listened as the male tried to convince the female to have sex on the bridge. He pleaded and used every line in the book—it was all we could do to stifle our laughter. She kept saying things like "I don't like it out here. Trolls live under bridges and people get murdered. Just like in the horror movies."

He continued to reassure her that the area was safe and he was actually making a little progress toward his goal. He said, "There's nobody out here for miles. Hellooo!" His voice echoed in the night.

My partner, who had a deep voice, howled back in his scariest voice, "Fressshhhh meeaatt!" The couple screamed in terror and ran for the car! They drove away fast, honking the horn for the other couple. We heard car doors slam down the road—but we were laughing too hard to know what was said.

—Robert J. Dykstra, detective lieutenant
Michigan State Police

Denny

I am not a religious person, though I am cognizant of unexplained happenings and the uncanny timing of certain events. My deepest questioning about "the order of things" occurred when my friend Denny Finch was shot and killed by John Clark, a mentally deranged individual.

John Clark's neighbor phoned 911. Something was wrong. John was pacing in his yard with a gun. She considered him dangerous and was concerned for her own and her neighbors' welfare. Denny answered the call and offered his assistance, since he had talked with John many times before.

When Denny arrived at the Clark's home, John was delusional. He thought the police were the Mafia and that Denny was sent as the hit man. Unknown to Denny or any of the local police, John had an arsenal of weapons and ammunition in his basement that included both automatic and semi-automatic long guns and pistols—even a .50-caliber sniper rifle.

I was finishing my shift and getting ready to unload when I heard Central Dispatch request a patrol unit to guard a neighborhood intersection. There were not many details given out over the radio, but I decided to answer the call. After sitting in the patrol car at the intersection for about forty-five minutes, I figured out there was a man with a gun and that police were evacuating nearby houses.

As I wondered what had inspired me to guard this particular intersection, I noticed an elderly couple walking their little dog. They seemed to be heading toward the standoff. Even though they were two blocks away from me, I felt compelled to stop them. I quickly ran up to them and said, "Excuse me, sir, ma'am. Please ..."

Before I could finish warning them, a barrage of gunshots rang out—so loudly and in such close proximity that I dove for the nearest tree! Suddenly I realized I was only ten feet from the gunman, who was standing in the front doorway of his house. I looked in back of me—*the entire police perimeter was behind me!* In my attempt to protect the couple walking their dog, I had put myself in the middle of a gun battle!

At that point, Denny backed out of the doorway and fell down backward on the porch. The deranged man was still standing in the doorway, with an assault rifle in his hands. I drew my weapon and fired several rounds at him. I knew Denny had been shot several times and I wanted to get to him. John disappeared through the doorway, so I thought I had hit him with one of the rounds from my gun.

The porch where Denny lay was about three feet off the ground. I quickly crawled to the edge, which had a thick railing around it. I was about twelve inches from Denny's face. He was moaning. I could see that he had been peppered with bullets from head to toe and that he was unable to help himself in any way. (I found out later he was shot twenty-three times.)

Denny begged me, "Get me off of this porch, *please.* I don't want to die like this. Get me off of this porch! *Please!*"

There is something about looking into a dying man's face and feeling his pain. I knew I had to do something. However, the only way to get Denny off the porch was to go up the steps, walk in front of the doorway, turn left, and then drag him back down the steps. The railing around the porch was so thick I couldn't possibly pull Denny through or over it.

I knew the suspect could shoot me—but the need to help Denny was greater than my fear.

So, I just did it! I was petrified. I counted, "One. Two. Three. Go!" I ran so fast up the stairs that I nearly broke my nose! I plowed into the side of the house before I turned left, then grabbed Denny under the armpits, and dragged him down the steps halfway across the front lawn.

I had wanted to move Denny in a "rescue carry" over my shoulder, but his one leg was almost severed. I was afraid it would fall off. His leg was only dangling on muscle and skin. Denny was not wearing a vest and he had been mercilessly shot up. I had to keep him close to the ground so his limbs would not fall off due to gravity.

At this point, John reappeared in the doorway. Apparently, I hadn't hit him—he had merely gone back downstairs to get another weapon as one of my bullets had jammed his gun. Fortunately, I had enough time to move Denny to safety. More gunfire came my way, but I was not hit. Denny was immediately transported to the hospital.

The doctors were able to keep Denny alive long enough so that his family and friends could see him once more and say good-bye. Even though Denny remained unconscious, his soul was still in the room. You could feel his presence before they turned off the life-support.

I'll never know what inspired me to answer this call for backup—but I can live the rest of my life knowing I helped a fellow officer get his last wish.

—*Todd M. Heller, detective*
Grand Traverse Sheriff Department, Traverse City, Michigan

A Sheepdog's Duty

Excerpt from the book
Promise Not to Tell by Alan L. White

April's bulging file lay on an already cluttered office desk, surrounded by student absence slips, class schedules, and two empty foam cups. April was about to begin classes at Clare Middle School. She was twelve years old and in the seventh grade.

The thumbnail photographs in her file depicted a happy child. Each image was of a little girl with blonde hair, blue eyes, and a crooked smile mugging for the camera. From kindergarten to seventh grade, only her gradual maturation showed—the eyes and smile remained the same. The large amount of paperwork the file contained was because April was continuously moving. Her seven years of education took place in seventeen different schools.

I ask the principals of each of my schools to notify me whenever we have a new student. I always meet with the child on his or her first day to introduce myself and explain what I do as a police school liaison officer. I offer the new students help in any way that I can and let them know how they can contact me.

April burst through the office door like she had attended the school for years. The two secretaries paused in their duties, a parent dropping off a student's forgotten lunch money stared, and I put aside my normally reserved first-meeting face and did my best to stifle a laugh.

April was a GLK In the Clare educational system, that means "Goofy Looking Kid." Her dirty blonde hair was piled high in 1970s fashion and held in place with a large plastic clip that seemed more suited for a bag of potato chips. Hanging from her ears and around her neck was an abnormally large and gaudy set of plastic costume-jewelry. April wore a low-cut flowered sundress, six-inch black high-heeled shoes that were at least three sizes too big, and a dirty-brown canvas jacket. When she walked across the terrazzo floor, she sounded like a Clydesdale on pavement and looked like a prepubescent version of the character Mrs. Wiggins from the Carol Burnett show. She'll never survive, I thought. The idea that in a few minutes this GLK would be walking into a junior-high classroom brought only one conclusion—they'll tear her apart!

April walked up to me and offered her hand. "My name is April," she said. "Are you the principal?" I told her who I was and what I did and a little about the school. Then, I offered to walk her to class. She said okay and walked behind me in silence up the stairs to her classroom. April was reaching for the door when I called to her.

"April," I said, taking a moment to choose my words carefully. "If there is anything that you need help with, anything at all, you can always talk to me." April tilted her head and gave me a "silly-boy glance."

"I'll be fine, Mr. White. Don't worry about a thing. I really am fine!" She gave me another quick smile and walked confidently into the classroom. As I walked back downstairs, I was overcome with the feeling that there really was something special about April. And I was right. Eventually, April would change my life.

It had been two days—two days of worrying about April and wondering why I worried about her so much. The e-mails from her teachers telling me that she was doing fine did nothing to placate me. I wanted to check on her. The bell rang for a change of classes and the hallways filled in seconds with adolescents in motion. I actually heard April before seeing her. It was the clomp, clomp, clomp of those oversized high heels on the terrazzo floor. "Hi, Mr. White!" April shouted from twenty feet away. She smiled and walked to me, still wearing the same flowered sundress, gaudy jewelry, and dirty tan coat.

"I just wanted to check on you," I said. "How are you doing?" I looked at her eyes, searching for any sign of trouble.

"You don't have to worry about me, Mr. White! I am doing fine. Promise!"

I looked at the throng of students milling around us. April sensed my fear. "I really am doing fine," she said. "I like this school and I am making friends!"

I looked back at her eyes. "Remember, anytime you need anything, just call. Okay?"

April gave her signature grin. "I know, Mr. White. You told me on my first day. Remember?" April shook her head and headed off to her next class. I left the middle school, no more relieved than when I first arrived.

For the next two months, I would check on April once or twice a week. Each time she would clomp up to me in those oversized shoes and wearing that same, but always clean, flowered sundress. She would say she was fine and not to worry. Each time I would tell her to contact me if she needed anything.

By the end of March, I did not need to say anything to April because she'd just walk up and say, "I'm doing fine, Mr. White!" In April, I decided that she really was doing okay and discontinued my biweekly visits, although I would run into her occasionally.

Another month passed. It was late in the afternoon and I decided to see her before I left for the day. When I heard April clomping toward me in the hallway, she smiled and seemed more upbeat than usual.

"Mr. White!" she nearly screamed as she walked up. Before I could respond, she reached into her purse and pulled out a folded piece of notebook paper. "Here," she said. "I wrote you a note. I colored the front myself!" The front of the note was indeed decorative. My name was written in bold hollow script that was intricately colored with a series of gel pens. I thanked April for the note and she clomped off down the hall. A school staff member came up and we began talking. I put the note in my coat pocket while we were talking and left the school shortly thereafter.

I was going on a fishing trip to my favorite trout stream. Spending the weekend with friends is what filled my mind as

I drove home that afternoon. After a busy week in the school, it was nice to think about fishing and great times around a campfire.

A couple miles from my home is a railroad crossing. The line of already waiting cars frustrated me as I stopped. It was while sitting there, anxious and frustrated that my departure was being delayed, when I remembered April's note and cursed myself for having forgot to read it. As I pulled out the note, I took a brief moment to enjoy the wide mix of colors and appreciate the time she took to draw this for me. I opened the note and began to read:

> Dear Mr. White,
>
> Hay, what'z sup? Not much here, just writing you a letter about me getting raped by my mom's boyfriend. It started 3 years ago at our house in Grand Rapids. He would wait till my mom was gone or was asleep.
>
> Then he would have me have sex with him. He would make me lay in the bed and take off my pants and shirt and then he would eat me out. When I tried to make him quit he wouldn't. The last time was Tuesday. He took me to the store to get a pop and candy bar. He got me a root beer & two king-size NutRageous bars and then took me to the park by the river. He drank one beer after the other. He told me that since I liked the song "Back Your Ass Up," to back my ass up, and then he made me have sex with him.
>
> The End.
> Love April

The car behind me honked as I put my truck in reverse and tried to move out of the line of cars. I worked my way around traffic and raced back to the police department. You could see my tire tracks on the pavement for almost six months after that day. I worked all night and did not go home until the man that violated April was in jail.

April moved again at the end of the school year. I never heard from her again.

I am now known as "Sheepdog." And it is because of this little girl, who until meeting me did not trust anyone with her pain, that I decided to dedicate my career to helping the victims of child sexual abuse. April forever changed my life.

—Alan L. White, patrol officer
Clare Police Department, Clare, Michigan

My Day in Court

It was an ordinary morning at the state police post in Bridgeport, Michigan. I was just getting ready to go for a lunch break with Bill Estlack, the court officer at the time, when Central Dispatch sent out a request for officers regarding a possible suicide. Bill and I decided to respond to the incident since we were nearby.

Dispatch advised that a distressed subject by the name of Allen had left a message on a friend's answering machine stating he wanted to kill himself. Allen's friend was concerned for Allen's safety. Allen could not work anymore due to a serious back injury and was apparently severely depressed about it.

When Bill and I arrived at an old dilapidated farmhouse, everything appeared quiet and serene. There were no vehicles parked outside, so we peered through one small opening on a garage window. Like many rundown residential buildings I'd visited, its windows were covered over with paper. We saw a pickup truck was parked inside.

Since there was a vehicle, we assumed someone was home. We knocked repeatedly on the front door, but got no answer. Since the call we were responding to was a safety/welfare check, we had no choice but to enter the house. It is always uncomfortable going into a stranger's house without first receiving permission. In this case, however, a man's life might be in danger, so we let ourselves in.

We checked all the rooms in the house and both of us called out Allen's name. "Allen, are you in here? Allen, where are you?" There was no response.

I noticed a door that was cut into the corner of two walls. At first it looked like a closet, because the door was locked with a simple clasp; but when we opened the door a couple inches and looked inside, it was actually a bedroom. We could see the soles of a man's bare feet on the bed. I said, "Allen, are you okay? Can we come in? We are state police troopers. We want to help you." As the door opened wider, we could see he had a gun.

I said, "Bill, he's got a gun! Don't go in there!"

Allen, who was half-dressed, sprawled out on the bed, and gripping a gun tightly in his left hand, yelled, "Go away! If you don't get out of my house, I'll stick this gun in my mouth and blow my head off!" Clearly, he was angry and in distress.

What we didn't know was that Allen had also taken a bottle of pills, which were perhaps impairing his judgment. He was slurring his words and moving erratically, so both of us knew something wasn't right.

Allen climbed out of bed, stood up, and staggered to the door. He was flailing his pistol as he walked. I can barely describe what this man looked like now because all I remember is looking straight down the barrel of his pistol, which looked like the opening of a cannon to me! As he stumbled toward us, he kept yelling, "Get out of my house! This is my house. I don't want you here! I'm going to kill myself, and if you don't get out, I will kill you first!" He seemed serious.

Initially, Bill and I tried to find a safe place to retreat to inside the house, but it was too small and cramped. There was no room anywhere for safe cover. There were piles of clothes and junk everywhere—but nothing that could guard against a bullet. Even though we had every right to shoot Allen, since he pointed his handgun directly at us, both of us resisted shooting.

We did not want to hurt him. Even though our guns were drawn in defense, we had come to save him. Bill and I made our way to the door and ran outside.

I believe Allen wanted us to kill him, and it did seem like a case where deadly force was justified. We were in danger. At the same time, though, we also knew this man was mentally ill and probably in terrible pain.

The emergency support team responded quickly to assist us, and, eventually, they talked Allen out of the house. At one point, however, Allen shot toward an assisting officer who was concealed behind the barn and covering the rear of the house. Bill and I were securing the front of the house while hiding behind a large oak tree. The assisting officer said, "That man took a shot at me! Can you believe it?" I was glad he wasn't hurt, but also that *my* tree was big enough for three people!

Ultimately, Allen was arrested for felonious assault on a police officer and escorted to the county jail. When it came time for his trial, both my partner and I were subpoenaed. I was one of the last witnesses called to the stand. I was a naïve two-year trooper and this was my first time testifying at an actual circuit court trial. The defense attorney badgered me on the stand.

He asked, "Well, if my client really assaulted you and pointed his handgun at you, why the heck didn't you shoot him?" I sat there for a moment, shocked at the question.

He added, "Aren't you a trained killer? Trained to shoot anyone who puts you in danger? Aren't you trained to shoot when a gun is pointed at you? If my client *really* pointed his weapon at you and was so dangerous, then why didn't you shoot your gun?"

It should be noted that in this type of an assault case, the prosecution has to prove to a jury, beyond a shadow of doubt, that this man did, in fact, point his weapon and threaten to kill us both. I knew Allen had pointed the gun at each of us, and I still remembered the "canon" pointed directly at my face! Nevertheless, neither one of us had chosen to shoot him.

I looked at the defense attorney, still in disbelief that he had asked such a question, and replied humbly, "I-I didn't take this job to shoot anybody!" You could have heard a pin drop

inside that courtroom. Then, I looked at the jury. I said, "My
job is not to shoot people. I took this job to help people. My
job was to save this man's life!"

Allen was convicted of felonious assault. And after twenty
years in the police business, I have never hurt or killed anybody. *I pray I never will.*

—*John Arthur, trooper*
Michigan State Police, Traverse City, Michigan

The Trooper's Daughter

Salmon swim up their rivers and wild geese fly south
in the fall, answering a call that logic has no part in.

Sunlight broke through the clouds and sparkled on the baby-
blue hood of her '68 Mustang. Katie had polished the car before starting on the trip, and it gleamed in the first sunlight
Katie had seen in a hundred miles. She set her jaw again, willing herself, making herself keep driving north. Tears of frustration came into her blue eyes. She wanted nothing more
than to turn the car around and drive back home, without
stopping. She wanted to be away from the state of Washington and race across the Columbia River, past Jantzen Beach,
to the safety of her apartment in South Portland. She continued to argue with herself, using the same line of reason-
ing that she had been using all morning, but to no avail. This
was something she had to do. She thought to herself, *Kather-*
ine Anne Olson, what in God's name are you doing? You are forty-
five years old, your own daughter is raised, you've got a good job at

the post office and a cozy apartment. Even your Mustang is paid for. What in the hell are you doing, wasting a Saturday, chasing a riddle? You grew up with no father. You raised your own daughter without a father, what are you thinking? If my mother got pregnant by a man who had no intention of being a father over four decades ago, so what? Drop it! But she couldn't. She had to know some things for herself, deep down, below the surface, where longings bleed quietly and questions nag, she had to know.

Since she was a toddler, Katie had struggled with questions like, "Why didn't my father want me? Why did he desert my mother after he found out she was pregnant?" She wanted to know what the old postcard in her late mother's personal letters file meant. The card was from a man named Lowell Dean Burt, and it had one line written in neat penmanship across the back: "Please reconsider." *Reconsider what?* thought Katie. Her dread about what she would find in Olympia had caused a knot in her stomach. She looked at her directions and took the Pacific Avenue exit. She wanted to drive slower, or not at all, as she followed Pacific down to Carpenter Road and turned right.

The postcard from long ago had a Tacoma postmark on it. Katie searched the Internet and found only one Lowell Dean Burt. She continued to search until she learned that he was living at the Roo Linn nursing home. She had called the office and was told that Mr. Burt was seventy-nine and popular with the staff for his humor and good nature. Rules at the nursing home forbid the nurse Katie spoke to from giving any medical details about Lowell to a stranger from Portland, but rules and the deep things of life are sometimes at odds.

The nurse had said, "I don't know what your interest in Mr. Burt is, nor did I tell you this, but if you want to see him, come soon. He has inoperable prostate cancer." Katie replied, "He ummmm, well, he might be my biological father."

It had forced Katie's hand that the man was dying. She did not have the luxury of putting it off until a later time. Two days later she drove to Olympia. She could see the nursing home on the right and she heard her mother's words in her head for the millionth time, "He left when he heard I was pregnant with you. He didn't want either of us." It was all the information that her mother would give her, despite her attempts to learn more.

Katie slowed the car at the entrance and put on her turn signal. She thought, *How stupid can I be? He didn't want me. He stayed out of my life on purpose. If this man is my biological father and I drove all this way to see him just before he dies, what then? I am a glutton for punishment!*

Katie pulled into the lot and parked the car. There was a double door going in with a big blue button that operated the doors automatically for people in wheel chairs. The smells of antiseptic, floor polish, and medicine hit her as she walked down the grey-blue carpet in the hall and passed by paintings of flowers that hung on the walls. At the end of the hall was a nurse's station.

She asked the nurse who was filling out a medical chart where Mr. Burt's room was located. The nurse, who was busy, looked up, giving Katie her full attention for the first time. Then, she took a too-long look at Katie's eyes, as if comparing her with someone she had seen before. "Two retired state troopers were in to see him earlier," the nurse said. "Yesterday, a state patrol captain was in to visit Lowell. The captain told me that Mr. Burt was the captain's coach when he first became a trooper. Lowell is almost gone, so please limit your visit." The nurse looked again into Katie's eyes, and Katie wondered if the woman could see the pain and fear she felt inside. "Stay as long as you like," the nurse told Katie as she went back to her chart. Katie started the long walk down the hall.

Old people looked out at her from several rooms as she came to the end of the hall and the door to room 113, which was closed. Katie knocked softly, and then pushed it open. There were two beds in the room, but only one bed was being used. Inside the room, she saw a small, shrunken man, sitting in a wheelchair and facing the window. His gaze was on the patch of lawn outside, where blue jays were fighting over some peanuts. He had a thin blanket over his shoulders. There were Christmas and get well cards on the wall. There were several pictures of Washington state troopers. On the table beside the bed was a plastic water pitcher with an upside down cup on top of it. "Mr. Burt, my name is Katie. I came to visit you." She pulled a chair up beside the small peaceful man and noticed that his fingers were shaped like her own.

He had liquid blue eyes that were familiar to Katie. She tried to make conversation with him, tried to get a feel of the man whose eyes and features matched hers. She felt a helplessness for both of them. She had come too late, known too late. She sat in the chair beside the quiet old man and finally let the tears spill across her cheeks and spread down across her blouse and onto her jeans. She gave herself permission to cry. The pain had to go somewhere.

After she had grieved for awhile, she remembered she had to use the bathroom and went into the private one in her father's room. Both rooms felt cold and when she walked back into Lowell's room, she noticed for the first time that only one of his feet had a sock on it. The bare foot was purplish with red veins, and when she reached down and touched the foot, it felt cold as ice. She looked on his bed and under his covers for the sock. Then, she knelt down and looked under the bed. She could see the sock had fallen down between the bed and the wall. She moved some boxes and a suitcase aside to make enough room so she could reach it. Her fingers found the sock and as she retrieved it, her eye caught something familiar on a shoe box under the bed. Rubber bands had been used to keep the box closed. Across the front of the box, carefully printed with a black marker, was the name "Katie." *He must have had a girlfriend named Katie, or a wife*, she thought. She knew she should leave it alone, but she couldn't resist bringing the box out with the sock. She put the sock on the frail man and the box on her lap as she sat beside him.

Her composure was coming back now. She knew the trip was pretty much a loss. She had, however, made the journey and now she forced herself to take it to the end. After the cry she had had, she felt a small amount of relief. *Well girl, you can leave anytime. You did the hard thing. If you want to snoop in this old man's box and read about some wife or girlfriend, go right ahead*, she thought.

With her new found freedom, there was also a fear of what she might find in the box. She took the rubber bands off of the box and removed the lid. The old man was still looking outside, at nothing in particular now, since the jays were gone. Inside the box were two wads of envelopes, each bound with rubber bands. The postdate on the top envelope of the first wad was December 15, 1960, and it had been sent from Portland, Oregon, ten days after she was born. The penmanship was her mother's. Katie's hands shook as she opened the worn envelope and took out a letter that looked like it had been folded and refolded many times.

Lowell,

You have a daughter. I named her Katherine. She has your blue eyes. Marrying you is out of the question. I never wanted a husband, just a child. If you come around, I will call the police. If you try to prove she is your daughter, I will deny it. We all have our stories, Lowell. My dad used me from an early age. I vowed to leave and never let a man into my life. I only dated you to get a child I could love, but not share. I never want to see you again, but I will send you a letter from time to time and tell you about her progress.

Helen

Katie's hands shook as she read her mother's letters to the old man who sat beside her in a wheelchair. They were informative only, and the letters had stopped when she was twelve. The nurse came to check on them. It had been two hours—a long time for a dying man to have company. She cracked the door open but closed the door again without coming in.

Katie read the first bundle and then let herself just sit and regain her composure. She watched him now, watched his features and considered his face for a long time, as he looked outside. From her changed perspective, she looked at her father with new eyes. It seemed to Katie that he was not watching blue jays and grass grow, rather he had an expectancy on his face, as if he was looking, waiting for someone and that if he turned away, he might miss them as they went by.

Katie picked up the second bundle and removed the rubber bands. Some dog-eared and stained pictures fell out from between the envelopes. All were of her, from her birth to about age twelve. Life, as Katie had arranged it for herself, had come totally unraveled in room 113. The things she believed in deeply and hated about her father were myths her mother had created out of her own hatred and deep-seated fear of men. Unconsciously, Katie had lived her life, much as her mother had. She had been divorced early on and raised a daughter on her own.

The first envelope in the second bundle was marked "Return to Sender," June 7, 1972. She opened it and pulled out the letter and read words and emotions that were foreign to her, things that she had longed for but had abandoned all hope of finding. It was a love letter in a way, from a father to his daughter. Her dad had asked her mother questions about his daughter, if she was okay, what she was like, asking if he might see her. It was about the time Katie's mother had decided to sever all ties with him. Katie was all her mother had and she could not survive losing her daughter to a man Katie never knew. The remaining letters had no postmark, because they were never mailed. Lowell had written his daughter a couple of times a year, dated the letters and put them in the bundle. A lifetime of loving a daughter he never knew were in the letters. There was a tenderness and a depth that Katie's mother never had, and there was an anguish that ran deep in the stream of every letter over his loss of his daughter. Katie read them, consumed them, like a person famished for food at a banquet. One by one, to herself now, she read the letters and cried. As she looked again and again at Lowell, her world was righted by the love this man felt for her. Three hours passed, three hours of healing and tears. When she came to the last letter dated June 5, 2005, she read it out loud:

My Darling Katie,
They say I have cancer. I have had a good life. I was a Washington state trooper. I stopped cars, rolled to wrecks and invested myself in my work and in the troopers I served with. It was my dream that you would be proud of me. I was strong once, vital and young. I met your mother in Portland. I loved her at once and I hoped to marry her. You were conceived and after she found out she was pregnant with you, she cut off all ties to me. Her father had done things to her when she was a girl that were dark and bad. I think she wanted you and not me. I tried to get her to marry me, but it only made her madder. So, when you turned twelve, she said you told her you wanted nothing to do with me. I was heartbroken. All of the birthdays,

Christmases we missed spending together. I hoped that when you grew up, you might want to learn about me. I am so sorry I wasn't there for you. I shed a lot of tears missing you. There is a tie between father and daughter that is stronger than the steel in the service revolvers I carried, or so it seems to me. My thoughts are that I love you and that I am so sorry I failed you.

Love,
Daddy

Katie couldn't see the letter any more through her tears. Sunlight streamed into the room and as she looked up, the old man turned his head toward her. He met her gaze with deep blue eyes. A cloud had lifted momentarily for him and for a few moments the old man's full faculties returned. He looked at his daughter with a look of love and tenderness that Katie would carry forever. "My girl, my darling daughter. I have waited all my life to meet you," he said.

Katie hugged him and repeated one word over and over, "Daddy." Then she said, "My mother lied. I did want to see you. I am so proud of who you are."

Healing came for both of them, and understanding and love flowed like full waves on an incoming tide, from father to daughter and back again. The aide brought them both a tray of hot food and they ate together and loved each other with their eyes and their smiles. When the aide came back for the trays, the old trooper sat beside his daughter, holding her hand.

It was later when a noise roused Katie and woke her. The room was darker now. She still held her dad's hand, but it felt different, colder. She turned on the light and saw him there, with a smile on his face. He was gone, his soul had ridden out on the last ray of sunlight, quietly, not wishing to disturb his sleeping daughter.

—Thomas A. Brosman, III
Senior telecommunications specialist, Washington State Patrol

It's a Bomb!

Report of a bomb threat in a large, crowded city park brings the Michigan State Police bomb squad running.

The alleged bomb is hidden inside a McDonald's bag that has been carefully and strategically placed on a park bench. Within minutes of the phone call, the entire bomb squad is in action. Big burly troopers wearing specialized suits and face shields drive the armored truck in to the park as close as they dare to the aforementioned park bench. In synchronized movements, they guard the perimeter and advise the growing crowd of onlookers to be careful. "Stand behind the yellow tape! This is a dangerous situation—come no closer!" Typical cop talk. Typical cop activity: guarding citizens at all costs.

The audience is transfixed as the bomb squad brings out the new robot (which the state police are *very* proud of, by the way). It is carefully brought into position by remote control—awesome technology to observe. The robot's arm is slowly and strategically extended toward the paper bag. It is just about ready to pick up the bomb to place it in the truck for detonation when, out of nowhere, a seagull dives toward the bag, snatches it up, and flies away with it!

The bomb squad started shouting and cussing at the scavenger. Some members grabbed their radios and tried to communicate with headquarters on how to best handle this change of events. Other officers scratched their heads in disbelief … and yet others started to chase the bird.

"Hey—follow that bird!"

"No, *shoot* it!"

"NOOO! We can't shoot it, the bomb will blow up!"

"If it lands in the tree, then shoot it."

"He's still flying, *dumb-ass!*"

"Uh, oh … oh no … he's landing …"

"Oh, NO! He's pecking at the bag!"

"RUN, Forrest, RUN!!!!"

Each time the bird landed, the crowd scattered in all directions. No sooner than everyone got situated and the gull would fly off again! The bird did this at least three times, as if only looking for a wee bit of privacy to enjoy its prize.

Since the bag had not yet exploded, Trooper Forrest finally said, "Hmm, maybe it's not a bomb …"

The bird eventually landed long enough to start pecking at the bag. As the bomb squad and crowd watched in anticipation, the seagull tore open the bag with its bill and pulled out a half eaten hamburger and some French fries! The empty McDonald's bag began to drift away on the breeze as onlookers laughed and clapped.

"Maybe you better chase the empty bag now, troopers!" Then someone offered, "I know—shoot the bird for *littering!*"

Embarrassed, tired, and silent, the state troopers began to load up the million-dollar robot. One of the officers picked up the bag and threw it in a nearby trash can.

If they hadn't experienced it themselves, this specially trained group of men would not imagine it was possible for one small bird to bring an entire bomb squad to its knees.

Thinking back, it was rather humorous.

—*Michael Thomas, captain, retired*
Michigan State Police

The Amazing Shot (with God's Help!)

My most memorable spiritual experience as a police officer occurred in 1990, when I was a member of the state police Emergency Support Team (ES Team). The ES Team manages crises for the agency and is called upon whenever a very dangerous situation requires extra support or specially trained personnel.

My team was requested to assist on a domestic violence incident. The situation had already escalated to two deputies down (both shot and lying behind their patrol cars bleeding) and a woman whose right arm was nearly blown off. She was bleeding to death inside her house. Her seventy-five-year-old husband, Gordon, had Alzheimer's disease and had shot all of them. He would not allow police to take his wife, though he did let EMS inside. They applied a tourniquet to the woman's arm, but she was gradually fading away.

As a team, we decided we would take a life in order to save a life. This was the first time the ES Team had ever made this decision. The team leader, therefore, was reluctant. Though the plan sounded callous, the man's wife was bleeding to death. Once the man was shot, the entry team could go into the house and extricate the woman to safety.

The lady was dying and our negotiation tactics were failing, so I volunteered to be the shooter. I was one of the best shots on the team. I could accurately shoot seven out of ten .12-gauge shotgun primers at fifty yards, with only a 4-power optical scope. I was good. (Primers are one-eighth of an inch in size.) I grabbed my 30.06 rifle and got into position. The plan was to call out to Gordon over the PA system, wait for him to cup his hands around his eyes, and then shoot him between the eyes when he looked out. He had already looked out the window like this several times. The front door had two long, narrow windows, each about eight inches wide, which are common on mobile home front doors.

We called to Gordon over the PA and, as anticipated, he cupped his hands and looked out the narrow window. I looked through my rifle scope, had a perfect shot, but suddenly I couldn't do it. I saw his elderly innocent eyes, his face—it was like looking at my grandfather! I lowered my gun and my spotter said, "What's the matter?"

I was somewhat stunned. I lied and said, "My scope fogged up." I raised my rifle again. During this moment of compassion and indecisiveness, I prayed to God that I wouldn't have to kill this man. However, a formal decision had been made for me to shoot him between the eyes. My prayer and my actions were contradictory. I reminded myself that our intent was to save the woman inside, so I aimed at the man's head and took the shot.

The man fell back. He never jumped, flinched, or turned. When the shot was fired, my scope and vision was dead-on Gordon's forehead above the bridge of his nose. I did not shake or shank the shot. The bullet hole in the window is proof. The hole shows where I aimed. If Gordon were standing upright again, the bullet hole was placed exactly between his eyes. And the shape of the hole shows the bullet went straight in.

However, the bullet actually hit his right shoulder, far away from his head. He lived! This is a bizarre and unexplained mystery. The crime lab went to the scene and measured. There is no explanation as to how the bullet hit Gordon's shoulder instead of killing him. The bullet experts could not explain how it happened, given the nature of the shot. The bullet hole in the window clearly went through the center of the window at eye level—and squarely! To hit his shoulder, the bullet hole would have had to have been lower and to the left.

Because police always want definitive explanations, several officers suggested that I just shanked the shot, but the bullet hole in the window clearly shows I didn't shank it. If I had, the hole would be in a different place.

God answered my prayer and moved the bullet. There is no other explanation. God, through the power of his own law, can do anything. This time, he defied the law of physics. The bullet must have moved after it went through the window even though, physically, we think this is impossible. Witnesses know Gordon never jumped up or swung his shoulder into the bullet.

Interestingly, immediately after the shooting, I could only see black and white. My eyes could not distinguish colors. Dr. Kaufmann, our departmental psychologist, said that I was in psychological denial because I didn't want to hurt anybody. I think my temporary color blindness was a symbolic message from God as well. After this incident, my vision about life changed from black and white to color, and so dramatically! This temporary visual impairment was indicative of the change in my spirit. I became more thankful, more grateful, and more spiritually courageous.

—*Thomas M. Curtis, lieutenant, retired*
Michigan State Police

seven
Weird & Freaky

There are some things that happen in police work—the weird and the freaky—that leave officers speechless.

Knocked Right Out of Her Shoes!

My partner and I work the 6 AM to 6 AM shift at the Michigan State Police Bridgeport Post. In January, around 10 PM, we were dispatched to a possible rollover PI (personal injury) accident on southbound I-75. Upon arrival, we observed a truck off to the side of the roadway, with a man sitting behind the wheel, trying to get the vehicle unstuck from the snow. Then, we observed a van that had crashed into the ditch about one hundred yards south of the truck. We proceeded to the van, which was occupied by three subjects when it crashed.

We also observed a third vehicle another sixty yards further south that had crashed into the median wall. As we were checking for injuries, I observed the subject from the truck staggering toward us. The female driver of the van stated the driver in the truck had been all over the road and she had tried to avoid him. The driver in the other car hit the back of her van while she was trying to avoid the possible drunk. It was a mess.

Back-up troopers arrived on scene and took care of the injured lady in the third vehicle. An ambulance arrived on scene and took care of the people with non-life-threatening injuries. My partner and I then focused on the suspect who appeared to be drunk. After we ran him through sobriety tests, which he failed miserably, we had a wrecker service dispatched and they started cleaning up the scene. They had the scene almost completely cleaned up and the ambulance had left the scene.

We were getting ready to take the drunk driver to jail, when I walked the one hundred yards north back to his truck. I told the wrecker driver that we were all set and no "holds" on vehicle, when we both looked across the freeway to the northbound side of freeway I-75. I saw a white vehicle in the left (fast) lane, gawking at the accident on our side of the roadway. The vehicle had slowed down to about 30 mph.

A black, four-door Blazer, traveling at the normal speed, hit the gawker's vehicle in the rear. It made a huge bang and then the gawker's vehicle hit the median barrier. The gawker's vehicle then traveled about sixty yards down the median barrier, shooting an impressive flow of sparks about ten feet into the air as it traveled.

At this point, I was irritated and let Central Dispatch know that we just had "gawker crash" on the northbound side.

Then the weirdest thing happened. I observed the driver of the Blazer get out of her vehicle, which was still in the left lane. The Blazer had a ton of front-end damage from hitting the gawker's vehicle, and the lights were not working on it. I looked and observed another vehicle heading *straight* toward the Blazer.

I started yelling at the driver to get out of the roadway, tried to get the approaching driver's attention with my maglight. I yelled at the woman, "Get the @#@# out of the road way!"

The woman made it to the passenger side of the vehicle's back door. The oncoming vehicle I'd been trying to stop crashed into the Blazer. The driver of that vehicle did not see the black Blazer and hit it at *full speed*. I watched the female driver "disappear" under the wreck and told Central Dispatch a pedestrian had been struck and I needed the freeway shut down right away. Then, I ran across the freeway and jumped the median wall.

I had to dodge a vehicle coming my way in order to make it to the Blazer. I observed a pair of women's shoes right where she had been standing and informed Central Dispatch that she had been knocked out of her shoes. To this day, I can't tell you where woman came from, but all of a sudden, she was standing up in the roadway! She was disorientated and staggering toward the right lane.

Then I observed two vehicles heading right toward her. I noticed she was wearing all black as she staggered into the vehicle's path. I started flashing my light on her, so the vehicles could see her. At the very last moment both vehicles parted around her like the Red Sea. One went off the roadway around her and the other vehicle went to the opposite shoulder. She made it to the shoulder of the roadway and fell to her knees, which is what I wanted to do also at that point!

I ran over to her just as another trooper arrived on scene to assist. The woman told me she was fine. I didn't see any blood on her at all. After her vehicle had been rear-ended, she got out to check on her friend, who was in the back seat of her Blazer. The friend was alright and both were checked out by EMS on scene. She was asked several times if she needed to go to the hospital and she stated she was perfectly fine.

The wrecker service took care of the other vehicles involved in the southbound crash and came back for the northbound vehicles. The wrecker driver, who stood right next to me as we witnessed the northbound crash, asked me, "So where is the dead girl?" I informed him that she wasn't hurt at all and his mouth fell open. We have no idea how she could have possibly survived the crash!

About a week later, I called the female at home to see how she was doing. She informed me that she couldn't remember much about the accident and didn't know what happened. I told her I'd seen her disappear when the vehicle struck the back of her Blazer. I told her that the vehicle hit her and her Blazer at full speed, and that I didn't know how she had survived. All she told me was that her back was sore and she had a big knot on her forehead.

I also told her I had seen her shoes, right where she had been standing, and that she appeared to have been hit so hard that she was knocked right out of them. Then she informed me that she had socks on also, but that she no longer had her socks on after the accident.

She didn't remember the two vehicles that almost ran over her either, as she was in such a daze after the incident. I told her this was the first miracle I'd *ever* seen like this with my own two eyes.

We never did find her socks.

—*Rick Jones, trooper*
Michigan State Police, Bridgeport, Michigan

The Psychic Janitor

I was conducting a polygraph examination on a subject named Rudy Oliverze. Rudy was a white male, who was related to a homicide suspect named Melvin Garza. Melvin was suspected in the disappearance of his girlfriend, Robin Adams, who was believed to have been murdered. The detective suspected that when the woman was babysitting for a friend, Garza came to the house, took the woman, killed her, and buried her. A few days elapsed before she was reported missing, so the investigation was cold from the beginning.

Rudy Oliverze was being questioned to see if he had information, involvement, or knowledge concerning the disappearance of Robin Adams.

We believed he might have helped Garza get rid of the body. During my pre-test interview, Oliverze told me that his real name was Raul Oliverze. In making conversation, he described his wife, Kathy. She had long blonde hair, parted in the middle, and pulled back behind her head. Oliverze failed the polygraph but made no admissions following the testing.

However, once he left the examination room, I found out that a detective from the Caro Post had been sitting behind the window watching the polygraph. The detective had been in touch with several psychics during the investigation, and one of the psychics—a janitor at the Gaylord State Police Post—had approached him while he was gassing up his vehicle at the post one day. The janitor told the detective about a dream he'd had, because he knew the detective was looking for a missing woman. (This conversation occurred well before I ran the polygraph.) Although the detective thought this was strange, he listened to the janitor because he was, indeed, conducting a homicide investigation.

The janitor stated that the woman was dead and buried. The psychic described a place in the woods that was down a dirt road. He said the detective would find the spot if he followed the road and crossed a bridge. He would then need to turn right and go up a hill. He was to follow a fence with unusual white signs, and there, in a clearing, is where the woman was buried. He said the woman was buried in the fetal position and she was lying on her right side.

This psychic janitor also described someone who could have knowledge or may have helped bury the body. His name was Raul Alavez. Oliverze was married to a woman with long blonde hair that she pulled back on both sides. His wife's name would be Karen. This man, Raul Oliverze, would have knowledge that would help solve the case.

The detective then told me that he did not know Rudy's real name was Raul Oliverze until he heard it mentioned during the pre-test interview I had just conducted. He said he recognized where the psychic said Robin Adams was buried, because he had visited the old grounds of the Caro Regional Center that morning. The white signs, fence, road, bridge, and clearing he had seen matched what the janitor described.

Later, Robin's body was found near this location—just as the psychic janitor said it would be. It was pretty freaky.

—*Charles Allen, inspector, retired*
Michigan State Police

The Flying Snowmobile

Houghton Lake is a large, beautiful inland lake in central Michigan that freezes over in the winter. The ice enables snowmobilers to "shanty hop" all over the lake, and the wide-open space allows them to accelerate to high rates of speed. In January of each year, I brace myself for Tip-Up Town, USA, an annual ice-fishing festival that attracts hundreds of snowmobilers to Houghton Lake.

One late afternoon, I was dispatched to a lakeside residence. It was a seasonal home that the year-round neighbors were watching over. The homeowners were not due back until spring. The house sets back about one hundred feet from the shoreline on a slight hill, with a large oak tree between the house and the lake. The tree is about forty feet from the water and adjacent to the house.

When I arrived, the neighbors were scratching their heads. A snowmobile, which was still running, was bucked up against the oak tree. None of the neighbors had approached the idling snowmobile. There were no footwear impressions in the snow leading up to the snowmobile or walking away from it. I thought this was weird. There was some damage to the front end of the sled, but no apparent damage to the tree.

My partner and I began to look for the driver. We imagined all the possibilities. Footwear impressions should have been evident—yet there were none. Thinking the worst, we walked down to the lake. Maybe the driver had hit thin ice and fallen through. I noticed an obvious snowmobile track that stopped just at the shoreline where there is a slight rise on the terrain, like a small snow bank; but nothing indicated the driver fell through the ice. We walked a huge circumference around the lake and the house, thinking the driver must have been thrown from the vehicle.

I walked back to the shoreline, looked at the tree, and then at the house in the background. I thought the snowmobile could have gone airborne after hitting the rise in the shoreline, especially if it was running at a high rate of speed. Then I saw damage on the tree trunk about ten feet up.

Suddenly I felt a small breeze brush across my face and happened to look up again at the house. The vertical blinds in the window appeared to move and I saw movement inside the house. It was strange that the blinds moved with the wind. There wasn't supposed to be anyone home.

I walked toward the house and saw a window was completely busted out. I moved a few blinds with one finger and peered in. Shattered glass was everywhere, but more notice-able was a man! He was dressed in snowmobile garb, lying half unconscious underneath the dining room table!

I quickly climbed through the window to check his con-dition. He groaned and moved as I made my way to him. I asked, "Are you okay? What's your name?" He had an injury to his head, there was blood dripping down his face, and his helmet was noticeably cracked. I gently shined my light near his eyes to check his pupils. When he groaned again I smelled intoxicants on his breath. I immediately called Central Dis-patch to send an ambulance.

Then I asked the man, "Do you even know what day it is?" I also urged him to stay still.

"Memorial Day," he groaned, rather indignantly.

Our accident re-constructionist said this was one of the strangest, most miraculous incidents he'd ever worked on. The snowmobile was, indeed, traveling at a high rate of speed. It went airborne at the rise in the shoreline, hit the tree, and then landed at its final resting place at the base of the tree. The driver separated from the snowmobile, probably at the rise of the bank, flying approximately one hundred feet through the front window of the house, blowing all the glass inside, and finally landing underneath the kitchen table.

Apparently, the driver entered through the window hori-zontally and parallel to the ground. His head hit one window edge while his feet hit the other edge, fracturing his skull and crushing both limbs. The blood, his condition, and damage to the house showed this. It was amazing he didn't hit the eaves and get his body sliced in two, or hit a smaller front window that was in his line of travel.

He was lucky to have survived.

—*Scott R. Bates, trooper*
Michigan State Police, Houghton Lake, Michigan

The Fatality

It was not uncommon for me to be twenty or thirty miles away from a call or an accident. One day the dispatcher reported a rollover accident—possible fatal—and requested for a car to respond. I radioed in and drove to the scene even though I was more than half an hour away.

When I arrived, I saw a car had rolled over onto its roof. There was no one inside. I did, however, find one body that had apparently been thrown from the car lying nearby, face up in the ditch. The strange thing is that the man's legs and arms were crossed. This was unusual. I couldn't help but notice how peaceful he looked. He was deader than a doornail, but he looked peaceful.

Fatal accidents require hours of tedious and time-consuming investigation. Pictures must be taken, sketches made, and measurements noted. The investigator may have to recreate the accident scene in a courtroom several years after the fact, so I requested assistance from an accident reconstructionist from the crime laboratory. *This will be a five-hour report before it is over*, I thought.

After I roped off the area and set out some flares, I returned to the car. As I was sitting in the cruiser, writing notes and recording data, an old Cadillac hearse pulled up. Two men were inside. They parked in front of me, waved hello, and smiled as they got out. I watched as they walked over to the body. Each man grabbed a limb and they started to carry the dead man toward the hearse.

To say the least, I was surprised. I jumped out of my car and raced over them. "What the hell do you think you are doing?" I bellowed. "Put that body back just the way you found it and get the hell out of here!" I made it clear that I had not summoned a hearse and wouldn't need them at least for a few more hours. I would call them when their services were needed.

The driver and the assistant stood there, dumbfounded. At six feet four inches and 225 pounds, they were not about to challenge me. They could see I was not in a good mood and meant business. They returned to the hearse.

After several minutes, one of them eased out of the vehicle and approached me. He said, "We were en route from our funeral home near Ft. Wayne, Indiana. We were transporting the body of a man who passed away the day before yesterday. We happened to come across this rollover just after it happened. Both the driver and one occupant were injured. Our hearse was full and there is more money in transporting injured people than dead people, so we put the dead guy in the ditch, loaded up the two injured individuals, and raced them to the hospital. Now, we are returning to pick up the original body."

I have had serious-injury accidents that turned into fatals; however, I never had a fatal accident that turned into an injury accident! Just goes to show, anything can happen!

Note: In the 1960s, just about every small-town funeral home used its hearse as an ambulance when they were not using it as a hearse. This helped pay bills and gave morticians something to do in their spare time. An Ohio state trooper, now deceased, shared this story with me.

—Michael Thomas, officer, retired
Flint Police Department, Swartz Creek, Michigan

Not Ready to Go

The police department I used to work for is located in a small historical town in southwestern Michigan. We would have occasional drug traffic on I-94 between Chicago and Detroit, but otherwise it was a quiet, uneventful retirement community.

One morning, my partner and I were called to a natural death at an elderly lady's home. The well-kept house was decorated with lavender Swiss-like shutters and surrounded by aromatic, colorful flower beds. I remember thinking what a pleasing place this would be to live.

When we entered the upstairs bedroom, we found several of the lady's relatives gathered around her bed, grieving and saying beautiful things about her and the life she had led. My partner had investigated many natural death situations before, but this was my first. Although she looked peaceful, she was obviously deceased.

I checked her pulse carefully, just as a matter of showing concern. She lay under the bed covers, wearing a soft paisley nightgown, with one hand on her heart—an unforeseen victim of a heart attack. We were told she was an active, spirited member of the community and highly vivacious. Although almost eighty, no one expected her to go this soon. I chuckled at the spicy romance novel sitting on the nightstand by her bed.

Her body was stiff to the touch and her face was an ash gray with deep lines indicating a joyful, happy life. I could tell she liked to smile. As usual, I lifted the bed covers to make sure nothing about the death appeared suspicious. While my partner continued taking notes, I phoned the coroner. The lady's daughter went downstairs to get us some coffee and give us space. We didn't object. It was a kind, warm environment. We were in no hurry to leave.

My partner bent over the body to check the carotid artery for a pulse once more—a standard procedure. I commented, "She's been dead over an hour. I don't know why we always overstress this crap."

At that moment, the dead lady's hand slipped off her chest and her chin and chest rose, as if to clear an airway from her throat to her heart. She took a deep, powerful breath, and then exhaled with seemingly deliberate intent! The breath was commanding, quick, and authoritative. We both jumped back in shock.

My partner dropped his pen and let out a suppressed shriek and said, "Oh *shit!* She's still *alive!*" His expression was priceless. I'm sure mine was, too.

After a few seconds of stunned silence, reality set in, and I regained my composure.

Defiantly, I leaned over her and as if I were talking to her ghost, I said, "Bull shit! You are dead. This ain't funny!" I inspected her face more closely.

It is not unusual for a dead body to let out gases and carbon dioxide, though this incident seemed well after the fact. According to the family it had been at least an hour since she died. I started to think the time line that they gave us was wrong.

No sooner had I finished talking when the dead lady suddenly took another desperate gasp for more air—sending me springing backwards in alarm, like a scared kitten, nearly tripping over my own shoes. I thought, *this is far from normal!* I exclaimed, "Holy shit! This is crazy. She is dead. This ain't right!" And then she took another frantic distressed heave for air.

I thought, *She's trying to resume her life again—or give me a heart attack!*

"It's-it's like she's trying to *jump start* herself back to life," my partner gasped. It was as if he had just read my mind.

She took a third breath, but discontinued in the middle of it. Then, as suddenly as she inhaled those two and a half breaths, she abruptly stopped. She exhaled and rested forever—as if realizing it was no use, too late, and her death forlornly inevitable.

My partner felt the same way I did. There was no reasonable explanation for the occurrence. The account is what it is. My partner and I left the room and indulged in a cup of decaffeinated coffee, while wishing it were Jack Daniels. We politely, but awkwardly, talked with the family members downstairs, but mentioned nothing about the incident. I did affirm she must have been a determined old soul who loved life to its fullest. My partner added, "I don't know exactly why, but I believe she was strong-minded, too!"

—*Anonymous, active-duty trooper*
Michigan State Police

eight
Signs, Symbols, & Synchronicity

In police investigations signs, symbols, and synchronicity play similar roles, turning up much-needed information through sources not otherwise available. Carl Jung's theory of synchronicity states that events widely separated in time and space cannot possibly come together by simple coincidence, but must be guided by another power. Whether one is a Carl Jung enthusiast or not, most police officers would agree that there is a peculiar gray line between pure coincidence and Divine intervention.

The Three Dogs

A few years ago, when I was in police uniform, I visited the local Humane Society. I was interested in getting a dog for companionship, as I had recently gone through a divorce and a work transfer. As I looked at the dogs, I thought to myself, *I'll adopt the first dog that comes up to me.*

As I wandered past the cages, I noticed a small shaggy mutt laboriously walk up to the bars of its cell and look at me. I thought, I know he is the first dog to come up to me, but I was hoping for a bigger dog, a manlier dog. I wasn't ready to commit, so I decided to think about it overnight and return the next day.

I decided to get the dog; however, the following afternoon, when I returned to the Humane Society, I couldn't find the dog. I thought, *Good, somebody took him home!* I went up to the lady to inquire. "I wanted that little dog that walked up to me yesterday. I thought he chose me as an owner. But I see someone has already taken him home."

Remembering me from yesterday, she shook her head forlornly. "I'm sorry, officer, but we put him to sleep this morning. He wasn't well. He had kennel cough and we couldn't afford to give him medicine or medical care. I'm sorry. I didn't know you were interested in him."

Streams of guilt and sadness reared their ugly heads, and I felt devastated that the dog was euthanized because of my hesitation. While still trying to recover from the unexpected shock, I decided to look at the other dogs. Somehow, on this day, the more manly dogs were no longer attractive to me.

Then I noticed another small dog that must have just arrived, because I hadn't seen him the day before. I could tell he was old and blind. He looked sad—kind of like me at the moment. He was curled up in the corner of his cell. He raised his head once and seemingly looked at me, but I doubt he saw me; his eyes were so milky.

The attendant shook her head in disgust, "Officer, it should be criminal what that family did. They owned that dog for seventeen years and then just gave it up to the Humane Society.

Apparently, they were moving. What were they thinking? How can people do that to an old, faithful animal? They should go to jail! It's just wrong. Nobody will ever take an elderly dog like that and he won't last much longer."

My chest thumped in discomfort as I compassionately looked at the old dog. I was trying to determine whether or not to adopt him. It was impractical ... the dog would need medical care ... he couldn't see well ... I already had the added stress of paying child support each week. All of these issues weighed heavily on my mind. The thought of bringing him home was out of the question.

The dog looked at me again and then gave up. He put his head down as if it was thinking, *Just go away. I may be old but I have dignity!*

Then a very old man with a cane walked through the door. He moved slowly and carefully. He saw the dog instantly. The dog looked up at the old man, but then put his chin back down. It was as if the dog was thinking, *Oh what's the use? Just forget it! I'm too old, crippled, and blind. Don't look at me like some freak! Why would you ever want someone like me? Go away! I know you won't take me either."* Then the dog closed his eyes and shivered like old men do.

Without hesitation, the old man said, "I'll get that old dog." My heart stopped, as if it was telling me, *See, dumb dumb! The old man listened to his heart and responded. Why didn't you? The heart is so much bigger and more intelligent than the practicality of your brain!*

The attendant said to the old man, "But, sir, I must warn you, he is a very old dog. He's blind. He has arthritis and needs shots. He ..." Her voice trailed off as I watched the old man shuffle up to the locked gate.

He spoke as if he had not heard a word she said. "I don't care about that. I want to get the damn dog! Look, he's all alone ..." She unlocked the gate.

The old man hobbled past the gate to the dog, which now stood up on all fours with some difficulty. The man insisted on picking up the dog. Briefly setting aside his cane, he managed to lift the dog with both arms. He said, "Hey there, old feller, your family died, too, didn't they?" The little dog lay his head on the man's chest, and I imagined that it was thinking, *Thank, God, someone came to get me. I'm going home now.*

As he carefully walked out the door, I heard him mumble to the dog, "Come on, old feller, we can grow old and die together—even if we only have a few months."

I was ashamed of myself and vowed I would somehow make up for these mistakes. I saw that the language of the heart seemed far superior to the practicality of my head and that the old man and the dogs had taught me something.

Two years went by. I never did get a dog and had voluntarily transferred to a police post five hundred miles north. It was bitter cold during the winter, but Lake Superior and the land were beautiful.

So, one day I parked my patrol car near the bay. As I ate a stale homemade sandwich for lunch, I watched the water lapping over the edge of the ice, which sometimes extended two to three hundred yards out. The wind was blistery and treacherous, kicking up the fluffy snow on the portions of the bay that were iced over. As I ate, I watched a few people congregating to my left. They were looking out over the bay, and I wondered what they were peering at.

I turned my car off and got out. I heard the most pitiful, wrenching, animal cry for help. In the distance, on the ice, was a small dog. I walked up to the group of people, all bundled up in their winter attire, but none was willing to go out on the ice.

Someone with a Finnish accent said, "We don't know whose dog that is, but we think it is stuck in the ice. We don't know how long it has been out there; we don't think he'll last much longer."

I heard the horrible howling cry from the dog again and couldn't take it anymore. I said, "I'll get that old dog," and started back to the patrol car. One of the bystanders said, "But, officer, the ice is really dangerous right now! Notice there are no ice shanties on the bay. You could fall through the ice…"

I interrupted, "I don't care about that. I want to get the darn dog. Look, he's all alone out there." I retrieved my snow-shoes from the trunk and put them on. The snowshoes were not required patrol car equipment but I was glad I had packed them. I also grabbed a shovel, just in case.

The snow and ice creaked under my snowshoes as I slowly shuffled my way to the dog. It appeared the dog had now lain down. As I walked slowly and carefully to the dog, I thought, *At least the snowshoes are wider and bigger than my feet and seem to be distributing my weight better over this ice.* The ice was, indeed, pretty thin.

After what seemed like forever, I reached him. I looked over the dog carefully. It appeared harmless and its eyes were closed. It was shivering, so I knew it was still alive. One foot appeared stuck in the ice. I started feeling déjà vu. I thought, *Have I been through something like this before?* The dog looked up at me but didn't seem to see me.

It was obvious the dog was in shock. It must have been out here a long time, because the ice was frozen around its foot.

I broke away the ice with my shovel and freed the dog's foot. Then, carefully, I picked him up and placed him inside my jacket. I said, "Hey there, old feller, where did your family go? Did they abandon you?" The little dog laid his head on my chest, exhausted, as if to say, *Thank God, someone came to get me. I'm finally going home!*

Slowly and carefully, I walked back to the car, knowing that we could still fall through the ice. I hoped that the dog was going to live. As I lay the dog gently inside the patrol car, I remembered the old man at the Humane Society. "Come on, old feller," I said, "maybe we can grow old and die together— even if we only have a few more minutes."

Fortunately, the dog made a complete recovery. Nobody ever claimed her. She looks to be a toy poodle.

—*A. A. Seller, detective sergeant*
Michigan State Police

A Trooper's Debt on Christmas Day

Brian sat in his patrol car on December 25, 2005. He was parked on a wide turnout on I-395, from where he could watch cars heading north out of Spokane. He was looking for DUIs and speeders and aimed his Falcon radar gun at cars that looked like they were "over." It was almost noon and there was a lull in traffic.

He put the Falcon on the seat beside him and turned up the FM radio. Christmas music was playing and Brian tried to count the number of Christmases he had worked as a trooper. He thought it was nineteen, counting the one he was working that day.

He had worked the first Christmases as a young trooper, because he needed the money. The later ones he worked so the younger men could be with their families. Ten service stripes on his shirtsleeve and the lines on his face marked the thirty years he had spent working the road.

For some reason, Brian remembered back to the big argument that had gone on in his family for years. It started when Brian was four or five years old. His mother was a devout Baptist and she figured that since Brian was her only son, he most certainly was going to be a Baptist minister. His dad, on the other hand, was a logger, who worked in the mountains between Colville and the Canadian border. He owned five logging trucks, two skidders, a big yarder, and had seven full-time employees. More than anything, he wanted his son to become a doctor—not a pastor—and for sure not a logger.

Dinner time is when the battles took place. Young Brian would take a bite of meatloaf or pot roast and scrunch down in his chair as the shelling began. "My son will become a Baptist pastor and we will send him off to Bible School. When he graduates, he can come right back here to Colville Valley and pastor a nice church, close to his mother!"

The big logger's face would get red and he would struggle to keep from saying something he might regret while he slept on the couch. "Woman, it will be a cold day in a hot place before that happens! That boy has the makings of a surgeon and I have not roasted and frozen in the woods most of my life to see my son live like a pauper. Doctors make good money and they get respect—not like a "gyppo" logger. When he is practicing medicine he can give lots of money to a church, but this boy is going to be a doctor!" The arguments took place at least once a week.

When Brian was eleven, his dad gave him a ring that was one of-a-kind. The jeweler in Colville who crafted it told Brian's dad that there was not another ring like it in the state. It had a wide gold band and in a strong setting in the center of was a large tiger eye stone. The jeweler placed the ring in a small box and as he wrapped it, he gave a few last words of advice to the logger. "I made the band man-sized, so he can grow into it. I will resize it for free if it's too big by the time Brian is eighteen. The tiger eye stone is supposed to bring courage, energy, and luck. It was worn by Roman soldiers for protection in battle."

Brian's dad waited until his wife was at the grocery store before he handed the gift to his son. "This is what a doctor wears, son. Keep it hidden until your ring finger is big enough to wear it. And don't tell your mother about this ring, even if she buys you a wooden pulpit to practice preaching on."

The summer of 1974 was hot, with lots of forest fires. In the early fall, the fire danger in the Colville National Forest was so bad that all logging was shut down for a couple of weeks. So, Brian's dad declared a holiday and the family left for Spokane on a warm Saturday morning. His parents were playing nice with each other; talking and chuckling as they passed by Deer Park and sailed on toward Spokane. The trooper who pulled in behind them paced his dad at twenty over the speed limit and turned on his light bar. The big logger rolled over to the side. The trooper walked up to the driver's side of the car and wrote Brian's dad a ticket for less than it should have been.

Brian watched every move the state trooper made and noted every detail of his uniform, hat, badge, and gun. He listened to the words the lawman said and how he conducted himself without arrogance, but with dignity. It was as if a hidden door opened for Brian—he knew beyond any doubt he had found his calling.

The next seven years flew by for Brian. By his senior year, the ring fit perfectly and he wore it with pride, picturing a Roman soldier, strong and brave, or a Washington state trooper. The battles for his future became wars; but even though his mom and dad were both stubborn, he was their son—and he had a double dose of resolve. He only grinned when they badgered him about his plans.

In late August, the letter Brian had hoped for came in the mail. His mother, with the look of a general who had lost a war, handed her son the envelope from the Washington State Patrol in Olympia. His dad's scowl grew as Brian opened the letter and grinned from ear to ear. Brian had been accepted as a cadet and his class would start in January. There were several months of wailing and gnashing of teeth by both his parents—but Brian became a trooper.

For thirty years he lived the life and wore the badge. Along the way, he lost his dad and his marriage. He had a daughter in Spokane whose husband was in Iraq. His daughter and son-in-law had a daughter named Ellie, who was eight years old and was the light of Brian's life. He adored the child, and she loved him back. She had named Brian "Paw Paw" before she could walk.

Brian broke out of his reverie and checked a passing car with his Falcon. He thought again about his folks and the turns in the road that life took. Sometimes, lately, he wondered if becoming a pastor or doctor wouldn't have been a better way. A trooper's life wasn't for everyone, though he had found himself and found his reason in it.

He had stopped speeders and drunks and been to a thousand wrecks, where without his help some people would have died. Many times he got blood on his uniform, trying to keep a victim from bleeding out or giving up. He remembered the one he called the "Christmas Wreck."

He'd been twenty-one at the time, with only two years on the job. A family was headed north on Highway 2, toward Newport, when the father lost control of the car on black ice and slid into an oncoming milk truck. He was the first on the scene. The trucker's injuries were minor since he sat above the car. The father was unconscious with a concussion and several fractures, and a passenger in the car, a woman, was in bad shape. At least one arm was broken and she was covered in blood. She had been cut by a shard of glass across her upper chest and her brachial artery was spurting blood. He'd gone around to her side of the car and, with hands as strong as the logger who sired him, put direct pressure on the gouging wound.

Far away, he heard the ambulance siren. When he saw the blood the woman had lost, he felt helpless and alone. What happened next made the hair on the back of his neck stand up. A small boy, maybe six, had been behind the passenger seat and was afraid to come out after the wreck. He was bruised, but had his seat belt on and was in one piece. The boy leaned over the seat and studied the trooper and his mother and father. Then, with words the young trooper would never forget, the boy prayed. "I call to you in heaven, and I know that you can hear me. I do not ask for myself, because I know that you will take care of me. I ask for my dad and my mother, that you help her to live. They need each other. Thank you." The little boy watched the big trooper, who was covered with his mother's blood, as his strong hand kept pressure on the wound. Eventually an ambulance arrived to take the victims to the hospital.

A call from Kim, the dispatcher, broke Brian's reverie. She asked Brian to call her back on his cell phone. He always laughed and joked with Kim, even in the most stressful situations, as a way to maintain sanity. Kim wasn't laughing or joking now. She was quiet and reserved. There was a long pause before she spoke.

"Ummm, Brian, I have some bad news. Your daughter and granddaughter were involved in an accident about a half hour ago. A drunk t-boned their car on the passenger side. Your daughter is in stable condition, but, ummm, your granddaughter has a punctured lung, several fractures, and internal bleeding. They don't expect her to make it."

Brian was shaking as he ended the cell call. He told dispatch he was en route to Deaconess Hospital. He noticed as he drove down Division Street that there were Christmas lights that he had never seen before. And he couldn't remember Gonzaga University being lit up like it was. He was in a slow-motion grieving stage. The best thing in the trooper's life would soon be gone. Ellie was the sun that rose and set in his life.

He parked his patrol car in the hospital parking lot and walked up to the ER. He found a nurse he had known for years and asked her to tell him the truth about Ellie. "Brian, she is in bad shape. The prognosis is not good. She will be operated on in the next hour. The doctor on duty is young, but he is good. I'll come find you when there is a change."

Brian walked numbly, putting one foot in front of the other, to the empty waiting room. The grieving trooper stood six feet-two. He was a mass of muscle and bone. He was a master marksman, and had never lost a fight—but as he sat in the deep cushioned chair he felt helpless. He covered his face in his hands as the worst nightmare of his life played on.

The place was empty. After a few minutes, he heard the voices of two men who were passing through on their way to a family gathering. They lowered their voices when they saw the grieving trooper and were almost out the other door when one of the men stopped in mid-sentence. "It's him! It's the trooper with the ring!"

Five minutes later, one of the men sat next to Brian while his brother, Dr. Ashley, scrubbed for surgery to operate on Ellie. Dr. Ashley was known by his peers as one of the finest surgeons in the state of Washington. For the second time in his life, Brian heard the voice, much older now, as a prayer was sent for help from above.

"I call to you in heaven, because I know that you hear me. It is probably not fair that I call on you to pay my debt, but this is not the first time. This is the trooper who saved my mother from bleeding to death. My brother, the surgeon, would not have been born a year later if it were not for this man. I am asking not for myself, but for this man, that you keep his granddaughter in this world. He needs her. So, I ask you to pay my Christmas debt. Thank you."

Pastor Ashley, who was pastor at the largest Baptist church in Spokane, sat beside the trooper, while three doors down his brother operated on Ellie. The surgeon labored, but so did his brother and also the angels, strong and kind, who came not to take her with them, but to bring her back.

Brian did not work on December 25, 2006. It turned out he needed most of the day—about six hours—to assemble the playhouse he bought for Ellie, and two hours for them to enjoy tea and cookies.

—*Tom A. Brosman, III, senior telecommunications specialist*
Washington State Patrol

Frog Time

I am a police polygraphist. A young woman with the weight of the world on her shoulders walked into my examination room one morning. She was pretty, but shy and introverted. At first, she didn't want to look at me. One of my initial thoughts when I shook her hand, was how sensitive yet powerful she was. And although little had been said—I already *knew*, somehow, she was truthful. As with everyone who enters my office, I gave her the benefit of the doubt and remained neutral. I could tell it would take time to gain her trust.

As we reviewed why she was there and talked briefly about her home life, thoughts of my grandfather, a man of Gaelic tradition, went through my mind.

My grandfather loved frogs. He said frogs had a beauty and magic behind their appearance. I remembered saying to my grandfather, "Oh, you mean like in fairy tales, when a princess kisses a frog and it turns into a prince?" He laughed and said, "Why, yes! Most fairy tales have some Gaelic tradition." My grandfather was a wise man. I didn't know why I had suddenly remembered all of this.

As the polygraph examination progressed, I could tell this young girl was different. I sensed that she was *aware*. I reminded myself that my sole purpose in being here, though, was to determine her truthfulness.

I allowed her to speak about her life, to share how she felt, and to give her side of the story. She was accused of stealing deposit money from a place where she worked. The case facts and circumstances seemed so clear that the employer had temporarily suspended her. The more I listened, however, the more she opened up, and the more I realized she probably didn't commit the crime.

The strange part was when she started to talk about a pet frog she had when she was younger. She said she loved frogs, but that she accidentally killed her frog one night when she forgot about him. She explained the house had become so cold when the heat went out that the water in the frog's tank started to freeze. When she finally remembered her frog the next morning, she found him frozen to the layer of water. She cried, then laughed, and finally said, "I don't even know why I'm telling you this ... maybe it's because I feel like that poor frog, frozen and unable to move. You're the only person who has listened to me and what I have to say. I really didn't do this crime! The facts look bad, I know, but I didn't do it!" She was teary-eyed, but sweet and sincere.

I reminded myself our frog connection had nothing to do with the *polygraph test* itself—but how freaky was this? I'd just thought earlier about my grandfather and what he said about frogs—and now she was telling me about a pet frog she loved that had died. And then she saw the frog's death as a metaphor for her own position—accused of a crime and unable to prove her innocence! I thought to myself, *Without even running the charts, I don't think she did this crime. I know I'm not supposed to judge, and I'll remain neutral ... I could be wrong ... but there is something just too weird going on here about frogs!*

Everything about the polygraph examination went smoothly. I showed her how polygraph works, and we ran a practice test. She was relieved, but still apprehensive.

I ran three charts total. I was fairly certain she was passing the test, but as always, I score out the charts when I'm finished. I do this in the same room with the subject, while continually watching his or her behavior out of the corner of my eye. She waited patiently, but concerned, as I scored each chart. I allowed her to get up and stretch. She drank her soda, and then sat back down.

Suddenly I saw the happiest, biggest smile on her face—like she'd had a sudden revelation or something. "What? Did I do something silly?" I asked, as I finished up with her chart evaluation.

Her eyes welled up with joyful tears, as she stared underneath the table, her head half-cocked as she strained to see something better. My chair seemed to be in the line of her vision. She looked dreamy. In a soft-spoken but jubilant and confident voice she proclaimed, "I passed! I know I passed the test!"

I gently smiled and said, "How do you know?" I knew she had definitely passed, but I hadn't given her my decision yet.

She giggled and said, "There's a FROG underneath your table—in the corner, half-hidden behind that old flowerpot..." Her eyes gleamed with inner knowing as she looked at me.

I spun my chair around and, sure enough, underneath the table was a ceramic frog—a beautifully handcrafted frog—that I had *never* seen before! I knew instantly my wife had put it there. She always said she'd surprise me with a frog one day, and she had visited the office a couple weeks ago.

I don't understand what to make of this synchronistic incident, but it certainly is a wonderful and mysterious concept. The young lady passed the polygraph test with flying colors, so I didn't *need* the frog thoughts to help me—though it did make this exam a little unusual.

On my drive home, I noticed a huge billboard with a red-eyed frog on it. It has probably been there for a long time, but I'd never noticed it before.

—*L.L. Bean, detective sergeant*
Forensic Crime Laboratory, Michigan State Police

Murder 101

Bill Brady, a pillar of the community and assistant quartermaster at the VFW hall, was dead. He had been shot six times. Unfortunately, there were no leads in the case. The victim was not involved in any criminal activity nor did he associate with people of questionable character. It appeared, in fact, to be the perfect murder. Everyone loved Bill very much, including his best friend, David Goldstick, who had found him dead.

A crime-scene investigator, Sgt. Steve Hickman, told me that the bullets that killed Bill were .380s, and I should be looking for a .380 in my investigation. I reviewed this information with my team and then we dispersed to conduct initial interviews. In response to a message I received from the Holy Spirit, I decided to interview David Goldstick myself.

As a police officer, I don't often talk about the messages I receive from the Holy Spirit because I don't want to be labeled by fellow officers as a "religious nut" or somebody "out in left field," but the truth is, the Holy Spirit of God gives me guidance and direction in my life. So, when the thought, *Interview*

David spoke to me, I selected David Goldstick as my person to interview.

I met David at the scene of the crime and asked him about the events that led up to his finding the body, his association with Bill Brady, and his family and friends. As we sat in the patrol car and talked, David came across as truthful and sincere. I was not suspicious of him at all. I also asked him if he had any guns. He answered, "No, my mom doesn't allow any guns in the house."

Afterward, when I was back at the office, I learned that David *did* have a gun registered, though it was a .357 magnum not a .380, like the gun used in the killing. The inconsistency made me curious, so I decided to ask him to return to the scene and be re-interviewed. He agreed.

As before, I talked with him in the car. David acted confused when I confronted him with the safety registration card. He swore he didn't have a .357—had never owned one. At this point, he seemed a bit uptight, but understandably so. He had found his best friend dead; that would be traumatic for anybody.

We were parked in front of the VFW building. There had been a fire there recently and the building was under construction. A makeshift office had been established next door in a pole barn owned by Bill's daughter and son-in-law. It occurred to me that the murder might be about money. When I asked David where the VFW's financial books were kept, he said in some filing cabinets in the office next door. Maybe money was missing and that was the motive for Bill's murder.

I asked David if the filing cabinets were kept locked and he said yes. I asked who had the keys. He said there were two sets. He had one set, and the other set was Bill's. I decided to secure all the information in those file cabinets so it could be analyzed. I asked David if we could we get the keys and he said, "Yes, we can do that."

At first he said the keys were in his house and then he said they were in his car, which was at a house where he worked as a caretaker; but then he said, "No, wait ... they're in my house." That is when I got the second major message from the Holy Spirit: *Obtain David's set of keys now.*

"What's at your house?" I asked.

"The keys ... maybe. Well, just take me back to my car."

So we took a four-minute drive to where he was working as a caretaker, turned into the driveway, and pulled up behind his black Jimmy. When I parked the car, David got out, and said, "Wait here."

What happened next I absolutely attribute to prompting from God. Instead of waiting, I got out of the car. I don't know why, other than I felt a strong need to get out of the car when David told me to stay. As he walked to the passenger side of the Jimmy, I walked up to the driver's side. The rear door window was rolled down about eight inches, and as I walked by it, I looked into the car.

The rear seat was folded down, and sticking out from underneath it was an object; it didn't immediately register what it was. After I looked at it more closely I could tell it was wood and that it had been cut. I immediately said to him, "Hey, can I look in your car?"

David said I could.

I opened the door and pulled out a sawed-off Rueger 10.22 rifle. The barrel had been cut off, a hose coupling had been placed on the barrel, and attached to that was a lawn mower muffler!

I've been asked how I feel when I get messages from the Holy Spirit. I can only say they just come to me. I only know that God is talking to me and that he has helped me solve many cases.

I held up the sawed-off shotgun and said, "What's this?"

He replied, "It is what I keep in my car. I take trips downstate, to Bay City and Ann Arbor, and I keep it in my car for protection." I spotted another box in the Jimmy and asked what it was. He said it was for silencing guns.

I went back to my patrol car and called for a marked unit. I wanted a warrant to search the Jimmy. My intention was to take David back to the VFW, leave him there, have the marked unit stay with the Jimmy and secure it, while I went to the Prosecutor's Office to get a search warrant. Before driving away, though, I took a short taped statement from David about the ownership of the rifle, the box and what he did with the box, and why these items were in his vehicle. I figured at some point I would need to deal with the gun being sawed off and the silencer being affixed to it. These facts were getting in the way of solving the murder since I knew we were looking for a .380, not a .22, but it was suspicious that he had the gun when he had earlier assured me he owned none. On the other hand, David was convincing about having the gun in his car for protection. He said, "I know I'm in trouble for *that*" and he nodded at the .22, "but I didn't do the other thing," which I took to mean the murder of Bill Brady.

It was a sunny day and David was wearing eyeglasses that darkened in sunlight so I couldn't see his eyes clearly, though it looked to me like there were tears forming in his eyes. I thought, *Are his eyes tearing up? Are they actually?* It seemed like they were, so as sympathetically as I could I said, "You know, Dave, a good man like you must have really had your back up against a wall to have done something like this..." He nodded his head affirmatively. As soon as he did that, I "mirandized" him. Technically, I didn't have to read him his rights, because I hadn't arrested him, but I obeyed the urge. I'm glad I did. I turned on the tape recorder and took another taped statement from David.

He admitted shooting Bill Brady. He took me to the murder weapon and the silencer box that was used and showed me the ammunition he had hidden in another vehicle in the garage at the house where he was a caretaker. The victim's blood was there, too.

Later, when we inspected the filing cabinet, I learned that David had embezzled a significant amount of money from the VFW and that Bill had figured it out and was going to turn David in.

Later, David's attorney said that my being so adamant about getting the keys to the file cabinet and finding the .22 and silencer were probably the turning points in our case and led to his client's confession. I have to believe he was correct. There were .380 casings inside the silencer box I had seen and David probably figured they would link him to the case.

Whether you call it intuition or being led by the Holy
Spirit, unexplained urges led me to solve this crime. It wasn't
great police work. I just listened.

—*Michael W. Wheat, detective*
Charlevoix Sheriff Department, Charlevoix, Michigan

Skunked

"Patrol desk, Anderson," I said after I punched line three.
"How can I help you?" It had been a busy evening. The phone
was ringing off the wall. I was alone at the desk—with the ex-
ception of the desk sergeant, who was sitting behind me reading the newspaper. For some unknown reason he felt above
picking up the phone and answering it. All six of the lines
were lit up.

Earlier in the day, a fourteen-year-old kid had raped and
murdered an eighty-five-year old lady on the city's west side.
They picked him up southwest of Lansing, but not before he
killed a policeman. The cop had pulled him over and the kid
just shot him in the face. A fourteen-year-old kid was a cop
killer. It's hard to figure.

"Just where in the hell have you been? That phone rang
more than twenty times. Is that why I pay taxes?" came a male
voice from the other end of the line. I listened to the man vent
his frustrations.

"What can I do for you, sir?" I asked when he finally took
a breath.

"Well, you can start by giving me your name. Someone's
going to hear about this! This is bullshit. The money I pay for

taxes and I can't get you bastards to even answer the phone!" He wanted me to apologize but that would never happen. Never apologize to a fool. He continued to ramble on and on.

"Hey, Anderson," came the dispatcher's voice over the desk monitor. "There's a lady on line six with a problem you can take care of. I told her we didn't have any cars to send her. See if you can handle it over the phone for me, will ya?"

I flipped the button on the console and said, "Yeah, sure. You might tell her there are five lines ahead of her." The dispatcher didn't respond.

"The name is Anderson, Richard Anderson. Badge number 324," I said. "Now, how can I help you?" There was silence. "Hello, you still there?" I asked. I still had five lines flashing.

"I want to talk with your supervisor," he bellowed.

"Sure, no problem." I put him on hold.

"Sergeant, line three is for you!" I went to line four.

"Patrol desk, Anderson," I said. "How can I help you?"

"Who's on line three? What do they want?" asked the sergeant, looking over the top of his newspaper. I ignored him. Several minutes passed, much advice was exchanged before I finally got to line six.

"Patrol desk, Anderson," I said. "How can I help you?" The lady on the other end sounded old. Her voice was shaky.

"Well, officer, I have a problem. It was such a nice day that I decided to open up the house and air it out. I opened all the windows and both the front and back doors. I saw it scamper across the back foyer, where the kids used to keep their boots when they were younger. Now, they are all grown up ..."

There was a long pause. "I wish Harold was here; he would know what to do. I just don't know what to do," she added.

"Well, where is Harold? When will he be back?" I asked.

"Oh, he's been dead for fifteen years now." All the lines were lit up again.

"Anderson, who's on line three?" demanded the sergeant. "It's not my 'ol lady, is it?" I cupped my hand over the phone and turned around to look at him.

"It's some asshole who wants to complain about the way I'm answering the phone, Sarge." The sergeant was well into the sports section of the paper.

"Well, I don't want to talk to him. Tell him something. Tell him to call back in an hour. Tell him anything."

I turned back around and returned to the old lady on line six.

She was still rambling.

"He took sick in the shop, Harold did, and he wouldn't leave to come home. Said he only had about two hours left. That was the way he was," she reminisced.

"Ma'am. Ma'am." I interrupted. "Listen, I need to find out what your problem is. Why did you call the police?"

"Oh, it's that thing in the basement. That thing that scampered down the steps," she advised.

"Well, what is it? Is it a squirrel?" I asked. "Just go down there with a broom and chase it back up the steps. It will run outside just as fast as it ran inside." I hung up the phone and pressed another line.

"Patrol desk, Anderson," I said.

"My husband just beat me up! Send me the cops!"

"Anderson, did you take care of line three yet?" asked the sergeant.

"Hell, no! He wants to talk with you!" I responded.

"Patrol desk, Anderson," I said into line five. "How can I help you?" It was the old lady again. She had moved from line six to line five.

"I wish to speak with Officer Anderson again, please." She remembered my name.

"This is Officer Anderson," I said.

"Sir," she began. "I'm afraid your idea is not going to work. I do wish my Harold was here. He would know just what to do. He was such a great man," she added.

"Ma'am, we just don't have a car to send over to take care of a squirrel in your basement. There are simply too many pressing emergencies going on right now," I advised. "I'm sorry, but that is just the way it is."

"Officer, officer," she interrupted. "This is not a squirrel. It's a skunk!" Shit. A damn skunk.

"Anderson! Did you take care of line three yet?" The sergeant was clearly annoyed. "It's still blinking!"

"No, sir, I sure didn't. I haven't had a chance," I answered.

"Well, take care of that asshole," he demanded. "I'm not going to talk to him."

"A skunk, huh?" I questioned. "Are you sure it's a skunk and not a cat?"

"Well, officer, I certainly know the difference between a skunk and a cat," she reprimanded. "If only Harold…"

"Yeah, yeah, I know. Harold would know just what to do, but he's not here," I said. "How about taking a can of something, like cat food or sardines, and make a trail from the basement up the steps and outside the house? Maybe the skunk will eat his way up the steps and outside. Then, just close the door behind him when he goes out." There was a pause on the other end of the line. All of the other lines were flashing.

"If only Harold were here, he would know what to do ..." repeated the old weak voice.

I took a chance on line three again.

"Patrol desk, Anderson," I said. "How can I help you?" The same gruff voice was on the other end. He had been on hold for over ten minutes now.

"I don't want to talk to you. I want to talk to your supervisor! I told you that an hour ago!" I put him back on hold and advised the sergeant of the call. This time the sergeant ignored me.

The hectic pace continued for two hours or more. One call right after the other. It was crazy. There must have been a full moon out that night. I punched line three again. "Patrol desk, how can I help you?" I asked.

"I wish to speak to Officer Anderson," said the old lady.

"This is Anderson," I said. There was another long pause.

"Your idea didn't work, Officer Anderson. I did just what you said and now there are two skunks in my basement." Two skunks. Shit! Now what? I was starting to wish Harold had been there because maybe he would have known what to do.

"Can you hold the line for a minute?" I requested and then put her back on hold.

"Hey, Sarge, you're a hunter, aren't you?" I asked.

"Sure, never miss a chance," he answered.

"Well, I was just getting ready to go grab a sandwich with Gillis. Can you take care of the lady on line three for me? It has to do with wild game." He agreed. I grabbed my hat and headed for the elevator.

"Yes, Officer Anderson is a fine lad," came the sergeant's voice from behind his desk.

"Harold? Well, where is he? When will he be back? Oh, I'm so sorry."

I had just reached the elevator door when I heard him say, "Sardines?" Then he yelled, "Two skunks?! Did you say two skunks?! Hey, *Anderson*!! Come back here!!"

The elevator doors closed. It started down. I was on my way to lunch. I smiled.

Gillis was parked out back waiting for me. We checked out of service with dispatch and went to a Coney Island restaurant for a sandwich.

"Would one of you be Officer Anderson?" asked the young waitress. "There is a phone call for you in the kitchen." I followed her through the swinging doors and picked up the phone. It was dispatch. They wanted Gillis and me to drive to a sheriff's department one hour away to pick up the fourteen year-old cop killer. We were to take him directly to the juvenile facilities where they would be expecting us.

I'll always remember the lad's face. You would have never guessed he was that young. He looked like a hardened twenty year-old. He reminded me of a caged animal. He was sitting in a cell on a bench with a straitjacket on.

"What's the deal with the jacket?" questioned Gillis.

"We can't keep him in handcuffs. If you put them on, he'll hand them to you in about thirty seconds," said the desk sergeant.

"I don't know how he does it but he does."

We kept him in the straitjacket and delivered him to the juvenile facility. The lady on duty at the detention home opened the door for us and was shocked when she saw the boy was strapped into a straitjacket. She ordered us to remove it at once. I reminded her who this kid was and that he had killed two people. My response fell on deaf ears. She assured Gillis and me that our supervisor would be hearing about this matter.

Gillis and I returned to the station. We were already two hours past our normal quitting time. The third-shift sergeant flagged us down. Sure enough, the lady was true to her word. "I've got an abuse complaint on you two. I'll need a report before you go home." We both sat down at a computer and wrote out a lengthy report. We explained our actions and the reasons we did what we did, always keeping in mind the possibility of a lawsuit.

When I was almost finished with the report, the desk officer yelled, "Hey, Anderson! Do you know what that Malone kid looks like or what he was wearing when you left him?" Gillis looked at me. I looked at Gillis.

"She let that little !&*&#@** get away, didn't she?" Gillis groaned.

The desk officer held his hand over the receiver of the phone and added, "He slipped away from the juvenile home just now. All Mary Poppins has to say is 'The little skunk just slipped away. Geez, I don't know where he could have gone.'"

Skunks. I'd dealt with enough skunks today already.

Gillis and I turned in our reports and headed home. It was now three o'clock in the morning. I wondered if the public had any idea what could happen in a cop's day at work.

My wife and I have a private joke. She uses it when she thinks I've had a bad day. She will ask me, "Well, what was the score last night?" and I usually come back with, "Well, we got shut out. One to nothing or two to nothing or whatever." We usually lost, but once in awhile we'd get lucky and score.

That morning was a different. When a cop gets killed, it takes the life right out of you. I hadn't even processed all that had happened yet. I poured milk on my oatmeal and just quietly replied, "We got skunked."

—*Michael Thomas, patrol officer, retired*
Flint Police Department, Michigan

nine
UFOs & Unexplainable Phenomena

This culmination of unexplainable phenomena addresses the "higher end" of the transpersonal perspective and may help to expand our grasp of what may be possible in the universe. Such encounters address the range of our potential for interaction and, thus, go beyond the person. It includes encounters with alien beings, UFOs, and shapeshifters, and any other anomalous phenomena. The nature of this chapter is not to prove or argue with these exceptional police experiences, but to simply keep an open mind and listen with deference.

Bizarre Weather

When I was a brand-new recruit at the St. Joseph Post, I was assigned to work with Larry Boger. Trooper Boger was a short, stocky, stubborn old man with a gruff voice, deep lines on his face, gray hair, and a cigarette in his mouth. He was the epitome of what we call "old school." I was green and shy.

We were having coffee at the local gas station when dispatch requested assistance on a train/pedestrian accident. This type of accident is usually fatal, so my heart started to pound. I had never been to a serious accident before.

We arrived at the train tracks in the area where a pedestrian was supposed to have been hit by the train. We didn't see anything immediately. It was a sunny winter day and the sky was blue. Larry advised, "Take your time and walk carefully down the tracks." (Larry always sauntered to my fast pace.)

As he grabbed the radio prep from the patrol car, I got out. These were the days when you had to have a "repeater" in the patrol car for the hand-held radio to work, and sometimes reception was poor. Larry was not overly excited, so I tried to copy his behavior. They always said in recruit school that new troopers are reflections of their senior officers. I wanted to act cool, stay relaxed, and be just like him.

Larry suddenly stopped. I thought to myself, *Oh my God,* but Larry remained calm. He put his cigarette in his mouth, took a puff, and slowly blew out the smoke. Then he matter-of-factly said into the prep, "Central Dispatch, we got a leg." My heart was racing, but I pretended to be calm. We continued walking down the track.

Larry stopped, put his cigarette in his mouth and took another puff. He looked up into the sky, and this time he blew smoke rings. He said into the prep, "Central, we got us an arm." His voice was monotone, and he seemed undaunted. We continued walking. Larry came to an abrupt stop. He had spotted something in the snow bank. He took another puff of his cigarette and said, "Central, we got us a torso now."

The snow was so bright I had to adjust my eyes. I was trying hard to see what he was looking at. In shock, I said, "Oh, okay. Now, I can see him!" I thought, *Wow, how does Larry stay so calm? I don't know if I can ever be like him.*

Larry looked at me and, like a teacher, said, "Now, young man, walk over there and see if he's alive. Check and see if you can get a pulse."

I was so sheepish! The torso lay motionless, its head partially face down in the snow bank. It was probably one hundred feet from the train track. I thought, *Holy mackerel, that poor guy had to be hit pretty hard to be laying way over here.*

As I approached the torso, I could feel myself hyperventilating. I was scared. I had never seen a dead body in this condition before. My pulse throbbed in my neck. Very slowly and cautiously I extended two fingers toward his neck to check for a pulse.

Suddenly, the man swung his body around, his face only inches from my nose, and blurted out, "Hey, I think I need an ambulance!" The man's eyeballs were nearly popped out of the sockets, like a freak at a Halloween party. I could almost touch the whites of his eyes!

I let out a shriek, jumped back nearly ten feet, and landed flat on my ass in the snow! Yes, it was a sight Larry and I never forgot.

The train had pushed and dragged the man at such a high rate of speed that his limbs were cut and thrown from the track in different directions. The man's limbs were severed so quickly and it was so cold outside that his blood coagulated and the man survived.

Two months later, I stopped him on the roadway for speeding. He proceeded to show me his prostheses! He was delighted to see me and enthusiastically said, "Thank you *so much* for helping me! *See*? I got a new arm and a new leg and I can drive!"

I decided not to give him a ticket. Somehow, it just didn't seem appropriate.

—*Anonymous, Michigan State Police,*
Detroit South Metro Post

Colors Never Seen Before

When I read the local newspaper headline "Mysterious Flying Object Might Have Been a Planet," I shook my head in frustration. I couldn't believe it. The unidentified flying object (UFO) I saw hovering over a lady's pole barn was *not* a planet rising over the horizon! I wanted to shake some sense into the local college astronomer who had suggested it. Even NASA engineers said the object was not a planet and gave their opinion that the metal was not man-made. I still have their report. And, fortunately, I had videotaped the event.

It happened one early morning just before Christmas. It was still dark outside, when my desk sergeant received a call from an excited, but frazzled, thirty-some-year-old woman who reported a "thing" hovering over her pole barn. She wanted to know what it was. I was dispatched around 6:30 AM. Both the sergeant and I admitted we thought the call was from one of the people recently released from a state mental hospital in our area. To this day, however, I regret not arriving at this woman's house sooner, when the UFO was closest to the ground.

After I took my time writing a citation for a typical speeder on his way to work, I arrived on her front porch, and knocked on the door. I wasn't too excited about this visit. The woman answered and appeared visibly shaken. "Did you see it? Did you see it? Did you see it when you pulled into the driveway?"

I said, "Nope. 'Fraid not." I was unenthusiastic. It should be noted that I am a fifty-year-old, cantankerous police canine handler and have been a trooper for many years. I am conservative, a member of the school board, and a Christian Protestant. I may not attend church regularly, and I smoke cigarettes like a fiend, but I'm a quiet-spoken, mild-mannered guy, who loves his family very much.

The woman urgently beckoned me in. "Then come in! Come with me! Right now! I will show you." She grabbed me by the hand and hustled me through the kitchen and dining room to the sliding doors at the back of the house. I stepped out on the deck and suddenly *my knees buckled!* I looked up and was shocked! I felt all the blood drain from my face, and my eyes must have been as big as tennis balls. Even my body started to quiver, which is very unlike me. I had seen some strange things in my police career, but *nothing* like this. This UFO was *massive!*

It was as big as half a football field and hovered silently above this woman's pole barn. Apparently, it had risen since she'd first spotted it—but I could still see it clearly. The colors were amazing. I was scared and excited, and the lady was grateful I had come as she requested. Later that day, even Paul Harvey said it was the wisest thing the woman could have done—to call the state police. I don't know if I would have believed just one person's story. As we found later, it became important that we had each other to talk to.

I radioed my sergeant and advised him that this sighting was no prank and that the woman had a legitimate concern. My voice rarely cracks over the radio, but it did that day. I know, you might think I'm a trooper gone wacky, but the object we saw could not have been from this world. It was too weird. I'll never forget how silent it was. It looked like the old-fashioned flying saucer in the *Lost in Space* television show, but the metal and its composition were different.

As we gazed up, we could see the bottom of it. It was a strange, ethereal, brilliant array of colors and lights, interweaving and dancing over and under each other; it's difficult to describe well. The bottom looked open and hollow. These brilliant colors and shapes resembled Honeycomb cereal, all woven together. That's the only way I can describe it. We commented to each other how the colors did not look real. They were colors we had never seen before—and they were BEAUTIFUL! I learned later that scientists believe there are other colors in the universe that we haven't seen with our eyes. I think we were true witnesses to this concept.

The lady had called her neighbor, Michael, just before I arrived. When Michael looked out his kitchen window, as she requested, all he could see was lightning bolts, radiating above her barn. He had put his robe on and walked over to get a look at it. I find it weird that neither Michael nor I could see the object at certain angles. It was only after Michael came over that he saw it, too. There was little to obstruct our initial views, from the driveway or from Michael's kitchen window, yet neither of us could see it from those vantage points. (Maybe this is what they mean by "cloaking" in science fiction.)

At first, the woman and I were going to try and assemble a new video camera that was wrapped underneath her Christmas tree, but then we decided we might not figure it out in time to videotape the UFO. So, Michael ran next door and retrieved an old video camera he had stored away. Michael videotaped some wonderful clips of the object, though it seemed to get higher and higher in the sky as time went on. The UFO was visible for almost two hours, from 6:30 AM to 8:30 AM. I can hardly explain how it disappeared from view. It was moving, but it wasn't. It just didn't seem real, yet it was clear as day to the naked eye and to the video camera. The UFO was completely silent the whole time, yet the lady's three dogs knew it was there! Perhaps it made a sound that humans could not hear but dogs could, or perhaps the lights affected them—whatever it was, they were petrified! Two of her dogs hid in the doghouse and would not come out when she called. A third dog, an Akita, hid under a bed in the house. Akitas are rarely afraid of anything.

After about an hour, three military jets flew over the top of the house, as if to inspect it. As the jets flew over, the lights went out on the UFO, and then they came back on once the jets were gone. I called my sergeant and asked him to check with the FAA, Camp Grayling, and any other military bases in the Midwest to ask why these Air Force jets had flown over northern Michigan. I know an Air Force military jet when I see one. To this day, the FAA and the military claim there were absolutely no military aircraft in our area. That is a lie! I believe our government knows much more than they care to admit or explain to common folks. I do not think this object was a military project either. People have suggested it was a military experimental aircraft, but I disagree.

We sent our video to NASA, whose engineers inspected it closely. Several of them actually called me and clearly stated the metal did not appear to be man-made. The lady, Michael, and I remained close friends after this sighting. Despite the amazing incident and the positive changes we experienced in our own attitudes about life—we had some mixed feelings afterward. The experience changed each of us in different ways. We talked about it for many years.

For instance, the lady, now my friend, chooses not to focus on the sky so much anymore. She is grateful to be living her life, here, now, day-to-day, and to be experiencing everything she has at the moment. She feels the incident and aftermath "grounded" her somehow. Michael felt much as I do. We no longer look at ourselves the same way as we did before. I'm more tolerant, open, and appreciative of the world we live in. The universe is so much bigger than I ever thought, and we are like little grains of sand. I now realize there is a higher purpose, a higher meaning in life that is difficult for man to comprehend. In fact, it's incomprehensible.

I believe the universe goes beyond our minds and our egos, and I am no longer as self-involved and self-absorbed as I once was. I watch and wonder more attentively now. I still see those colors dancing in my head and wish I could share them with people. Our universe does have colors we've never seen before.

—*Written in loving memory of Glenn Guldner, trooper, deceased*
Michigan State Police, Traverse City, Michigan

This story was written by Detective Sergeant Ingrid Dean, in memory of Trooper Glenn Guldner, who shared this personal story with Dean before his death. He provided Dean with the still-shot photograph of the UFO from the videotape he created. The other male witness involved in this sighting is also deceased. Both men died from cancer. Only the female subject still survives but prefers to remain anonymous. Some people wonder if the men got too close to the unidentified flying object and if it possibly emitted radiation that affected their health.

The Encounter

I retired from the police force in 2002. The encounter occurred in the middle of the night in September 2008 at my home in a rural area near Holland, Michigan, which is on the coast of Lake Michigan. It had been a warm, calm, uneventful evening. My family was in bed, and the last thing I remember is that I was sitting on the couch watching TV.

The next thing I knew, I was standing in the yard outside my home. It was dark and very quiet. I was not dreaming; I was completely conscious. The silence was eerie. Ahead, in the near distance, I saw a pin-size light and then a very bright wave-like flash that seemed to move through and past me. It almost knocked me back a step. Then I felt a presence behind me, and when I turned around to see, there were three small gray beings just standing there—shoulder to shoulder.

They were the classic gray, four-feet-tall aliens that are commonly seen in science-fiction movies and books. They had large black, almond-shaped eyes and long slender arms and legs. Oddly enough, I was not afraid, and I did not feel intimidated in the least. It was as if I somehow knew them.

The being in the middle said they needed my help. His lips did not move. Communication was telepathic, and I heard his request as if it came from a friend or neighbor. I willingly agreed to help. I don't remember what happened next, but the next thing I remember is looking up and seeing a huge craft hovering. There was a second craft about four hundred feet away from the main one, and I sensed that time had passed since I first communicated with them, but I couldn't tell how much.

I was in a semi-paralyzed state and very tired—as though I had done a lot of work—my breathing was heavy, and felt damp with perspiration. It took all of my strength to just stand up. My arms hung down at my sides, and as I looked up at the craft, I noticed something out of the corner of my eye. Using all the strength I could muster, I looked to my left and saw two men (humans), whom I didn't recognize, standing near me. We were about ten feet apart from each other and looking up. They appeared to be in their thirties. Neither of them seemed able to talk and they looked as paralyzed and tired as me. They were breathing heavily, too, and there was no sound to be heard nor a breath of air moving.

A bright light at ground level was behind us and illuminated the area, including the craft hanging in the air; but I couldn't turn around to see the source. Then, I realized the small gray beings were gone.

The next thing I remember was looking up at the craft in the night sky. There was a thunderous sound and an opening two- to three-hundred-feet wide appeared in the sky. It was amazing! I could see blue sky and clouds through the opening—but it was still night time where I stood. Clouds were "turning into themselves" around the opening.

Then, in the blink of an eye, the first craft flew into the opening, followed instantly by the second ship. Then, the sky closed up.

Again, I heard a clap of thunder. With that, I awoke from this strange state and found myself inside the house. However, my eight-year-old daughter was now sleeping on the living room floor, which was weird. *What the hell just happened to me?* I wondered. I grabbed my kids' crayons and start drawing what I saw.

I noticed it was about 5:30 AM. At this point, I was in a daze. My wife went to work, my daughter to school, and I didn't share my experience with anyone. As usual, my wife called me from work later that day.

She told me that our daughter woke up around 3:30 AM and saw a lot of bright flashing lights outside our roof dormer window. My wife told her to go back to bed but instead our daughter went to sleep on the living room floor.

My jaw dropped when my wife told me this because I had not said anything to her about what had happened to me. I had now received some confirmation that my encounter had really happened.

Later, I talked with my daughter about that night and she said she saw about eleven flashes of light. That's all she counted before she got scared and put her head underneath the covers. She waited a little while before looking again and, when she didn't see the lights anymore, she ran up to tell her mom.

If my daughter awoke between 3:00 AM and 3:30 AM, and I found myself back inside the house two hours later, what happened to me during those two plus hours? Why did I feel so tired? And, most importantly, why couldn't I remember anything in between? I was sick with flu-like systems for a week, which was odd because I seldom get the flu—especially at the end of summer.

I filed a report with the Mutual UFO Network (MUFON), and they have been supportive and helpful. MUFON said that I'm one of only a few people who remembered the hole in the sky. They also said it's not unusual to only remember the beginning and the ending of such an experience.

Two scientists came up from Detroit and Indianapolis to do exhaustive testing and a complete search of my property. They inspected a small tree in the backyard that dropped dead only one week later. They also found some plants dying off and they took soil and leaf samples. I have not heard anything back as of this time, and I believe the investigation is still ongoing.

Not a day or an hour that goes by when I don't think about this experience. It doesn't run my life, but I constantly replay the incident over in my mind. It was an extraordinary experience, one I never thought would happen to me; but it did, and my life will never be the same.

Afterward, I felt driven to make a model of the UFO. I also designed a rudimentary picture of the hole in the sky. The craft had vein-like lines going around the outside of the main sphere. These red veins had a glossy appearance. The two smaller white globes on the ends of the beams seemed to glow slightly.

—*Kent Milner, reserve officer, retired*
Grandville Police Department, Michigan

Burnt Offerings

Excerpt from *Burnt Offerings* by Charles W. Newsome

In Santeria religion, there exists a dark side called Palo Mayombe. The Palo Mayombe originated from the African Congo and is said to be the world's most powerful and feared form of black magic. Individuals who practice this dark aspect are called Palero. The man being chased by the officer in this story was a Head Chief Palero in the Palo Mayombe. He practiced extremely strong and powerful black magic. He killed babies in rituals and was wanted by the police. He was known to be a shapeshifter.

The Palo Mayombe has a very long history. This magic was transported to the Caribbean during Spanish slave trade to Cuba and Puerto Rico in the 1500s. There is said to be a big difference between Palo Mayombe and Santeria. The religion of Santeria uses the forces of light. The members of the

Palo Mayombe use forces of darkness to achieve their goals and magic spells. Because the Palero practice such powerful black magic, many members of Santeria avoid being associated with Palo Mayombe. Some members of Palo Mayombe have migrated from Cuba to the United States.

———

I was about thirty yards away when a porch light came on at a house on Junction Street in response to my partner's gunfire. It was only by chance that the subject turned momentarily in response to the noise and saw me. I could see in his look that the shock nearly turned him to stone. His throat erupted in a primal scream of rage—or was it fear? I knew at that moment that never before in his life had he felt the humiliation of that emotion. He tossed away the rifle he held in his hands and bolted. Even as he coursed along the fence row, his legs pumping furiously, I put myself in his mind and could almost hear his thoughts, *How had this happened?* He'd no doubt been chortling in self-satisfaction over being able to find my partner and me sitting unsuspecting in the unmarked scout car, and to sneak up—so he thought—behind us so easily. Then I came upon him from behind, and found him in the dark. I could almost hear him shout, *Why, by the blood of Zarabanda, didn't I feel him approach?* But he must have forced the distracting thoughts aside, because he pelted furiously toward Junction, with me in close pursuit.

A fence enclosed the western end of the field he'd been hiding in, so I doubted he would head that way—a man might climb a fence when he came to it, but it would slow him down. I sensed that he would head toward Junction. I was right. As I lurched into stride and raced after him, I heard more shots reverberate from the direction of Merritt Street, where my partner apparently engaged an accomplice. No matter now. Nothing I could do. The chase was on. The subject emerged from the field and ran onto Junction. He crossed the street and continued eastward on Merritt, skirting another warehouse on that side of the street. I was only twenty paces behind, but I wasn't young anymore. At forty-three, my wind was no good. He began to pull ahead.

I was still only thirty paces behind when he reached the far corner of the warehouse and turned left. In the time it took to take two breaths, I reached the corner behind him. Despite my ragged breathing, I grinned with satisfaction. I knew this building, and I knew that the subject had fled into a blind alley—there was no outlet, the high walls of the storage buildings rose on all sides. The alley ended in an impenetrable wall of cement. He was trapped. As I paused at the corner of the building for the barest fraction of a second, I eased my head past the brick façade just far enough to peer with one eye down the alley. I was stunned. The cul-de-sac was deserted. The subject was gone! I thought at first that my eyes were deceiving me. I looked again, my whole head emerging from behind the wall. Nothing. I stepped quickly out and walked warily down the alley, my .357 Magnum revolver at the ready. Had some workman left a door ajar, permitting the subject to escape into a building? What rotten luck! But no, as I remembered, there were no doors, just the walls of the buildings ... and the roofs were twenty feet in the air. I walked all the way to the end of the alley, my eyes searching in every corner and crevice. There were no parked cars. There were no trash dumpsters. There were no stacks of crates. The alley stood as clean and empty as an airplane hangar. There could be no mistake—the subject had simply vanished.

I holstered my weapon and stood for a moment in the dark alley, letting the silence fill me. The cold, the sense of malignancy were gone, but a trace of something intangible lingered in the air. It was a faint smell, so ethereal that I wasn't sure it was really there. I sought it, tried to identify it, and finally lost it.

After a while, I smiled and walked away, returning to Merritt Street and my partner, who was thankfully alive and uninjured after a shoot-out with one of the subject's associates.

Only when a lieutenant and an inspector arrived, took charge of the homicide scene, made notifications, and started asking questions, did I break out of my reverie and start talking to Magaly, the New York City magazine reporter who had been riding along with my partner and me for over a week.

"Where have you been?" she asked, breathless, her hair disheveled. She was completely out of sorts over the shooting she'd witnessed only moments earlier.

"Chasing someone," I said. "Chasing our guy. It was *him*. I know it. But he's gone. He got away. Disappeared."

Looking into her eyes, I could tell it was impossible for her to gauge my mood. She finally said, "Well, it's dark. It'd be easy to lose someone ... I guess it happens, huh?"

"No, I mean he *disappeared*," I insisted. "He just vanished, Maggie. He ran down a dead-end alley. I had him. I really had him. He was cornered. Then he was ... *gone*."

"Well, he couldn't just—"

"He did." I turned again and looked into the night. "He did."

Maggie shivered. "It's him, then," she murmured. As you say, Bill. It's *him*." I quietly nodded.

Before the arrival of the homicide team, the lieutenant, with the consent of the inspector, took initial steps to preserve evidence and organize the scene. First, I ordered a scout car crew to go back up to the vacant lot where I had discovered the subject hiding and secure the area. They quickly found the rifle the subject had thrown away, nestled among some weeds. They let the weapon lay where they found it, and waited impatiently for it to be photographed, measured, and ultimately retrieved and tagged by responding evidence technicians.

Next, the lieutenant requested a K-9 unit to come out to the scene to attempt a track of the subject. The dog handlers arrived within a few minutes and were directed to the waiting officers along the fence line in the vacant lot. The dog, a big German shepherd, immediately picked up a scent from the ground, as well as from the rifle. He pulled eagerly at his leader and struggled against the leash, pulling his handler along at a trot. "Find him, Rocky," urged the handler, a young cop whom, Magaly said, looked like Andy Garcia. "Find him, boy!"

The dog followed a strong scent all along the route I'd taken in pursuit of the subject, all the way into the dead-end alley, and down to its end. The dog sniffed nervously along the blank wall for a moment and then sat on its haunches, staring straight ahead—it was trained to do that after locating the person it was looking for. Rocky was doing his job. "There," he was saying.

"There he is—in the wall."

I never saw the subject again, and no arrests were ever made.

—*Charles W. Newsome, sergeant, retired*
Detroit Police Department, Detroit, Michigan

The Lost Badge

A young Canadian conservation officer in Sault Sainte Marie, Canada, shared the following experience with me as I was crossing the border into Michigan. I noticed he wasn't wearing a badge on his jacket and I curiously inquired about it. He pulled his badge from his pocket and stated, "See, I do have a badge, but let me tell you what happened." He then relayed this extraordinary story. I am a practicing police polygraph examiner, and I totally believe him.

———

I wanted to kick myself. What kind of a police officer loses his badge? But that is what I'd done. And, in the middle of the woods, of all places! I searched and searched, but it was a losing battle. The thick layer of fallen bark and leaves was an ideal place for a badge to remain hidden. Every time I thought I saw something, shadows would move across the ground, revealing that what I had seen was only a glint of light filtering down through the leaves. Nevertheless, I returned to the woods the next day and the next, each time retracing my steps, even getting down on my hands and knees ... but to no avail. It looked like I would have to break down and report the loss of my most treasured possession.

Reluctantly, I decided I would make a report today; after all, somebody else might find it and use it illegally to impersonate a police officer. My cheeks burned as I thought about the ribbing I would get from everybody at the Ontario Provincial Police Department when they learned that I had lost my badge. But an unexpected assignment prevented me from sitting at my desk and writing up my report.

A severe storm had ripped through the northernmost section of Ontario, more than one hundred miles away, and I was asked to travel there to report on the extent of the damage. I still hadn't given up on my badge, and as I drove north I said a prayer that I would find it.

When I arrived at the designated area, I found old mossy trees, pines, limbs, and brush had fallen everywhere; the forest was chaotic. It looked as though the wind had lifted most of the trees up and thrown them down into piles of debris. I noticed an eagle's nest had toppled, and the tree in which it had been built was nearly upended. I thought, *What if there were baby eagles in the nest?* I felt a strong urge to investigate. If there were birds in it, I could transfer them to a wildlife refuge.

Carefully I picked my way through black timber, rocks, fallen trees, and brush, climbing and tripping as I made my way awkwardly through the devastated landscape. I expected the worst and thought I would find the mother dead and her eaglets injured, starved, and thirsty, or perhaps the whole family would be dead.

To my surprise, the nest was empty! I sifted through the leaves and bark—mother and babies had vacated the nest, and there was not a sign of disaster to the family. Relieved, I stepped back to admire how well the nest was put together and how cleverly constructed. This was the first time I had seen an eagle's nest close up. Just the fact it had come down intact seemed a miracle.

And that's when I glimpsed something shiny sparkling through the leaves and sticks. I picked into the lining of the nest, and there, nestled safely inside, was my badge!

For a moment, I couldn't believe it. To say that I was astounded would be an understatement. I thought I was dreaming. The eagle had recognized a treasure and carried it to the safest place she knew, her home. And I, concerned about the safety of her children, had found it.

What was the likelihood of such a sequence of events being just coincidence? How was it that I was the person chosen to drive one hundred miles to a forest previously unknown to me? If the eagle had not found my badge and carried it off for safe-keeping, perhaps I might never have seen it again. And why did I feel such an urge to look inside the nest?

What humbled me the most was the complex series of steps I had been led to take. And I didn't even know it when I took them!

—*Vernon R. Petersen, detective lieutenant, retired*
Police polygraph examiner, Michigan State Police

The Kid

Abandoned mines are extremely dangerous to explore, or even to go near. In Utah, many are undocumented, especially on private property. Mine shafts are particularly hazardous because they are nothing but vertical openings that go very deep, some more than one thousand feet into the earth. People can fall into the shafts never to be found again, which makes abandoned mines and mine shafts ideal places to dump dead bodies.

I am a federal undercover officer and my work requires special clearance. A confidential informant told me that a body had been dumped down a winze of an abandoned mine shaft. Winzes are vertical drops, but within the mines themselves they are shafts that connect one level to another lower level, like an elevator shaft without the elevator. Winzes can descend to depths that are water-filled, toxic, and radioactive. I'm sure bodies can decompose quickly if culprits know what they are doing. (I do not recommend anyone ever explore such places. The shaft collars of these dormant mines are often loose and unconsolidated and the sides of the walls break away easily from intrusion.)

I drove into the quiet countryside and got permission from the owner to investigate the abandoned mine on his property. I first searched for any disturbances in the area— such as loose gravel, footwear impressions, and blood— anything to indicate that a body was dumped. I didn't see anything unusual. What I did find was old equipment and piles of waste rock all around a couple of old buildings. I spotted what I believed to be a mine tunnel; it was wide open. At least, this was consistent with what the informant told me. You can't always trust an informant's information.

I shined my light through the mine opening and could see movement in a dark corner. It appeared to be a child, about four feet tall. I immediately yelled to him, "Police, come out! You are not in any trouble! It is too dangerous for you to go any farther! Hello?" There was no answer.

I thought it might be the rancher's kid, but learned later that he didn't have any children. This was a desolate area and it didn't appear like anyone had been here in a long time—not even vehicles.

Reluctantly, I stepped into the opening of the mine. I didn't intend to proceed much farther; it was too dangerous. The opening was held up by old support timbers that seemed safe enough and stable, but they could easily have been rotted wood. I tried not to be fooled by appearances. Such old structures can easily disintegrate from the weight of just one person "Young man," I said, "this is NOT a cave! It is unstable and can cave-in! Come out!" I felt anxious for the boy to walk out as I knew the dangers of these places. Still, no answer.

I walked into the mine a little farther, and I could see movement again. "I see you! Come out! I just want to talk to you. You can DIE if you fall down a hidden shaft!" There was no answer—yet I knew I was not seeing things. It had to be a kid. It moved on two legs and appeared agile. He moved quickly.

I was certain the kid was playing games with me. Then, I thought to myself, *Okay, I'll just be totally still and catch you on your way out. Then, I'll give you a good scolding and send you home.* I stood behind a support beam for what felt like an hour; in reality, it was probably only twenty minutes. It was a hot day and time felt like it was standing still. Then, I saw a flicker of movement and the shadow again, but as soon as I saw it, it disappeared. I swear I didn't move a muscle.

I started to second-guess myself and think, *Well, it could be an animal. Maybe it is a bear or a mountain lion and is merely escaping the noon heat. After all, animals are known to den in these mines.* I kept one hand near my pistol at all times.

It must have been 100 degrees, even in the cooler recesses of the mine. I took a drink of water and saw the movement again. The shadow was definitely two-legged and there are two obvious, long, slender arms. *It is human alright*, I think. I no longer doubt myself. "Come on!" I shouted. "I could use your help right now! Talk to me!" It moved swiftly again from one support structure to another. I couldn't see it clearly in the dark. I stood still for another twenty minutes. I had decided to wait until it was close enough and then shine my flashlight on him. Admittedly, I was hot, getting frustrated, irritated, and tired of waiting. Nevertheless, I remained motionless and unwavering.

When I'm truly beginning to doubt myself again, I finally saw more movement, and now it was getting closer. He was almost within arm's reach; I had him now! I surprised him. I shined my light on him in one swift click of the button. When he turned toward me, I saw a *reptilian-faced creature* that scared the shit out of me—and I ran! The instant the light shone on its face, it dove into the earth like it was water. Initially, I thought he went into a winze, but there didn't seem to be an opening, though it was dark. The ground was solid where it had disappeared.

I wasn't seeing things. Its face was greenish-gray and reptilian. Maybe it was an animal, but no one has been able to convince me of that yet. It was too weird! I suppose it could have been a person in a mask, but in a dark mine? With no one else around?

—*Anonymous, retired*
United States Army, Special Investigations

Flying Free

I was dispatched to an accident on a country road about five miles out of town. A sixth-grade teacher on her way home from school ran over an eleven-year-old boy on a go-cart. She was driving fifty-five miles an hour.

The child's family lived on one hundred acres that were intersected by the highway. His parents bought him a go-cart and built him a track. Half of the track was on one side of the road, while the other half was on the other side. They instructed their son to always stop before crossing the road, and he had promised to observe this rule. Unfortunately, on this fatal evening, the boy forgot to stop and look before crossing. He was hit by an innocent motorist and apparently thrown from the go-cart.

When I arrived at the scene, the driver of the vehicle, a middle-aged woman, was frantic and hysterical. She started running to a nearby field. "He's over there! He's over there! I saw him go over there! I saw him fly from his go-kart into the field! Oh, God. He must be okay. He must be," she sobbed.

The teacher darted into the field, just off the roadway, and I obediently followed close behind her.

"He's over here!" she called. "I know he is! He's somewhere in these bushes." We began running in circles ... round and round ... nonstop. We could barely keep our breath. The lady, now delirious, kept saying over and over again, "He's got to be here ... he's got to be. I *saw* him fly over my windshield. He's here ... I know he is."

Suddenly, I had a horrific thought. It somehow wound its way through my own confused and anguished mental state. I said, "Stop!" At first she didn't seem to hear me. I ordered her again, "STOP! This is insane! Stop running!"

She was panting. I was panting. I listened to my inner thoughts, now coming through as clear as day. *The boy is under the car.* I looked to the roadway and at the teacher's car and said, "He is not here. He is under the car." We proceeded to walk back toward the road.

She protested, "But, but ... but ... I saw him *fly* into the field! He can't be under the car. He was here ... he flew over there!" And she pointed behind us.

As I already intuitively knew, the boy *was* under the car. He was dead, probably killed instantly. I do not, however, believe the lady *imagined* seeing the boy fly into the field. I think what she saw was the boy's soul departing his body. He was struck so fast and with such force that he flew out of his body instantly.

Looking back, I realize we always have a choice to buy into another person's energy. We were running around in circles like maniacs—until I took control and said, "No. This doesn't feel right." When I quieted myself, then a clear message was able to come through.

Sometimes police troopers buy into energy, just like other people, but we have to learn to listen for spiritual guidance even more closely during emergencies and tragedies.

Angels can't help us if we don't listen.

—*Robert I. Arciniega, trooper, retired*
Michigan State Police

Swimming Out-of-Body

One early morning in late October, Central Dispatch received several 911 calls from various Lake Leelanau residents. People could hear a man screaming for help from across the lake. I stopped at one of the residences to look, listen, and better pinpoint the man's position. Although I could hear him, it was still dark, so I used my flashlight to scan the water.

I finally located the distressed man in the water about one hundred yards from shore. He was barely clinging to his capsized fishing canoe and still screaming. He had been doing so for at least forty-five minutes. Without any further delay, I dropped my gun belt and stepped into the frigid water. I was an excellent swimmer, having grown up in southern Florida, but this was different. Not only was the water freezing, I was also wearing a polyester uniform, a bulletproof vest, and black boots that added weight and discomfort to my rescue efforts.

The man kept yelling, "Help me! Hurry up! I can't last much longer! H-E-E-L-L-P M-E-E-E-E-E!"

Because my adrenaline had kicked in, I finally shouted back crossly, "Shut the hell up! I'll be there in a minute!"

I ripped off as many unneeded items as possible and started to walk toward the man. I thought to myself, *Piece of cake. I won't have to swim too far, this is shallow water* … Then, without warning, I went from chest deep to sinking to above my chin before catching myself and treading water. The drop-off was so unexpected I accidentally inhaled freezing water.

My body went into shock. It felt like someone had squeezed my chest until it was the size of a ping-pong ball. I had never had an out-of-body experience until now! My whole respiratory system stopped, just like that, and I could see myself treading water. For a few seconds I became the panic itself.

I can hardly describe what it felt like when gallons of ice cold water started to fill up my uniform. I was shocked that my boots floated, while my vest weighted down my chest. My arms were already going numb, but I started dog paddling. I splashed and kicked backward until I reached shallow water again. (God sure gives us some excellent survival instincts.) Then, I stood up.

I still felt separate from my body and was trying to recompose my bearings and thoughts. I thought to myself, *Now get it together. You threw your own wrench in the situation by not being careful. Regain your faculties and swim out there again! It's okay. Just slow down.*

Sometimes, I don't know if these are actually my own thoughts or if God is talking to me. I finally thought, *Okay,* and then I started swimming toward the man. I noticed the yelling had been reduced to small, intermittent, helpless yelps with long intervals in between. I was concerned he was going to go under.

No sooner had I reached him, when he passed out. This was a good thing, actually! I knew I wouldn't have to combat any resistance as I towed the man back to shore. It was exhausting! Visually, the distance seemed far, but near water, distance can be an illusion. Somehow, recruit school training didn't match what I actually felt in a survival situation. For a big guy who works out, this was one of the most physically challenging feats I'd attempted. When we got to shore, I was so tired and cold that everything seemed dream-like and to be moving in slow motion. It was weird seeing life like a dream!

At first, I was so relieved to be on shore. I thought, *Thank God! I made it to shore and I see people! Someone will help me now!* I could see fire trucks and EMS personnel scurrying about, but then realized nobody was coming to assist me. I could hardly stand up, let alone drag the man any further!

Suddenly, I saw a huge piercing light and was blinded! It was still dark out and the bright light stunned me. I carefully dropped the fisherman to the ground and stared blankly into the light. No, it was not an I-see-the-light-I-must-be-going-to-heaven situation. I was just confused! It took me a few seconds to see clearly, because I was in shock. As I adjusted my eyes, I saw a volunteer rescue worker just standing there, shining his blazing flashlight at me, only inches from my face.

I yelled at him, "Damn it! I've already seen the light once, go grab us some blankets!" I probably shouldn't have been so hard on the young fellow. He was apparently very new to his job.

When I got home, I peeled off my uniform and I learned that polyester is the worst material to swim in because it retains every molecule of water possible and no heat whatsoever. It took me three days to feel warm again. The man did survive and fully recovered from the incident. I was awarded a Medal of Honor by the Michigan Sheriff's Association.

—*Duane Wright, deputy*
Leelanau County Sheriff Department, Michigan

The Golden Shield

During the summer of 2004 at 0230 hours (2:30 AM), my patrol partner and I were doing routine patrol. While on traffic patrol, one of our units noticed a vehicle parked in the wood line of Pike Field. When they approached the vehicle, they had the driver step out and then they started questioning her on why she was parked in the wood line. While they were talking with the driver, a male stepped out of the back of the vehicle. The patrol was unaware of this male and had not looked inside the vehicle.

The male walked up the officer who was asking the driver questions regarding her parked vehicle. The officer asked the male to step away until he was finished speaking with the driver. The male did not take this lightly and attacked the officer.

Luckily, this patrol was a two-man patrol unit. Unfortunately, his partner was used to working the desk and not the streets. The partner placed the male suspect in a full naked-choke hold. The male jumped up and dropped backward onto the officer, and when the officer hit the ground, his weapon came free from his holster.

Upon hearing the gun hit the ground, the male subject quickly picked it up. Both officers took cover while the subject held the gun up in the air and yelled, repeatedly, "What are you going to do now?"

The first officer then called over the radio "10-33 (officer needs help), subject with an officer's gun!" When the dispatcher heard this cry for help he responded, "All patrols 10-33 Pike Field!" I then hit the lights and started that way, knowing I was a good five minutes out, going 10 mph over, so I requested to run code three. When I received clearance, I then knew I could make it in about two to three minutes.

When I was about forty-five seconds out from the scene, I noticed a dim golden light shielding my vehicle. Then, a voice rang out so softly, "Do not fire, no one will be hurt." Upon arriving on the scene I noticed I was the second patrol unit there, and that they attempted to use a four-ounce can of OC spray on the suspect. The spray wasn't having any effect on the subject.

Just before I climbed out of my vehicle, I noticed the golden shield was brighter and covered all of the patrols on scene. I heard the voice again. It said, "Do not fire, you will be fine." As I pulled my weapon out, I had the subject in my line of sight. He started waving the gun around like a mad man. So far, he had not pointed the gun at anything but the sky. As I approached the rear of the lead vehicle, the subject looked up at the gun and then dropped it. He fell to his knees, not saying a word, or even making a move other than breathing.

After apprehending this subject, the golden light vanished like it was never there. It was such a strange phenomena and I'd never seen something like that before.

The next day was a range day and I had to pre-qualify with my weapon. While out at the range, I cleaned my weapon and lubed it up to be fired. At the firing lane, we were instructed to fire the first ten rounds. When I pulled the trigger nothing happened, not even a sound came from the weapon. The hammer went forward, but nothing happened.

When I cleared the range, I took the weapon to the arms room and had it checked over. I learned that the firing pin was broken and the guide rod was bent. The guide rod spring was damaged. I don't know how this happened because I take very good care of my weapons.

The arms room, to this day, does not know what happened to my weapon either. The weapon had just been inspected two days before the range and was fine!

I'm not sure who or what the voice was, nor do I know what the golden light/shield was all about, or where it came from. I was sure glad it was there, though! I hate to think of what could have happened if my weapon did not fire on the scene.

After that event, I never asked anyone if they had seen this golden light or heard the voice. I didn't even tell my partner about it, due to what he might say. I am glad that someone has finally given me a way to share this incident without judgment.

—*Jonathan Matteson*
Military Police, United States Army

UFO Sighting

On January 8, 1956, I was stationed at the Michigan State Police, East Tawas Post, near Wurtsmith Air Force Base, in East Tawas, Michigan. I worked as a road trooper on night patrol. My partner, Max Waterbury, had talked to me about UFOs just days before this incident, which I thought was eerily ironic. He said anyone who believed in UFOs was crazy and should be put in a mental ward.

At the beginning of our shift, we stopped for coffee at the local restaurant near the state dock. East Tawas is located on Lake Huron. Our lunch was interrupted with a telephone call from the desk sergeant at our post.

Wurtsmith Air Force Base had called the state police post to request that troopers check on a large object that had been hovering about 2,000 feet above Strawberry Marsh. The air base had it on its radar and had been watching the object for the past half hour. The military officer was excited but concerned and asked us to take a look.

Max and I hurried back to the post to pick up a few things, including a rifle that Max grabbed out of the closet. I looked at Max and said, "I thought you didn't believe in unusual objects or little green men. What if they're friendly?" He just rolled his eyes, and we left.

Strawberry Marsh, a rural deserted area with driving trails and unoccupied hunting camps this time of year, is halfway between East Tawas and Oscoda. The snow was at least two feet deep. I plowed and barreled our patrol car through drifts and undulating terrain, until we finally rested in a three-foot snow bank. In my trooping era, whoever got the car stuck had to shovel it out. The right front wheel seemed to be the side that was up. I was bent down and shoveling a combination of snow and wet gravel, when Max, who was standing in back of me, excitedly exclaimed, "Look at that!"

I turned around, looked up, and then dropped the shovel in surprise. My eyes were nearly blinded. In the clear night sky, I observed a huge oval-shaped light fringed in red and green floating above the snow-capped tree line. It appeared to be hollow, but wasn't. We were shocked. We knew that if this object was hovering at 2,000 feet, as the military radar operator explained, then it had to be *massive*. From our 45-degree observation angle, it looked about fifty feet wide. We couldn't believe what we were seeing. It wasn't a beam of light, but rather a brilliant, bright light that illuminated everything below it. The stars were out, but there was no moon, which lent well to the brilliance and clarity of the lighted object.

I am a private pilot and have owned six different aircraft. What we saw was no airplane of any kind. What we thought was so weird was the *silence*. It didn't make a sound. As we watched, it would move back into the tree line where we could barely see it, but then move forward again into our view. It was *huge*.

I grabbed the radio and talked to Trooper Warner Palmer, who was working the desk that night. Still shocked, I reported our encounter, and I told him, "This thing is *huge!*"

Trooper Palmer sounded just as excited as I did, answering, "Right! I got the Wurtsmith Air Force Base holding on both lines. Your description is consistent with theirs!"

As the object disappeared behind the treetops—this time for good—I was able to successfully free our patrol car from the snow bank. The base advised that they'd vectored a T-33 to investigate, so we headed straight back to the post. We learned later that they had been watching and tracking this object for at least an hour. I typed up our report and left it on the front desk counter for the media to pick up in the morning.

We were not the only officers who saw it. Deputy Leon Putnam from the Iosco County Sheriff Department had also seen an object from his patrol car that night. He had made a traffic stop and was writing notes inside his vehicle when the object illuminated the interior of his patrol car. He described it as a flaming basketball, however, hovering over the treetops. His description was not the same as ours.

My partner and I were told that the Air Force would never call troopers at the post again. Apparently, the air traffic controllers who dispatched us were "pulled on the carpet" and got in serious trouble for having contacted us. When reporters from the local newspaper tried to interview the commanding officer, Colonel Taylor, he told them, "No comment." The military denies to this day that anything unusual happened. They denied ever sending a T-33 to investigate.

This incident occurred when all three major newspapers in Michigan—the *Free Press*, *The Detroit News*, and the *Times*—were on strike. I had hoped the sighting would reach the wire services, but it never did.

Later, Max humbly asked me, "So, what do you think that thing was?" He never ridiculed UFOs again.

—*Raymond Bronicki, trooper, retired*
Michigan State Police

The Fall of Light

During the summer of 1973, I was stationed in South Dakota and assigned to the 44th Strategic Missile Wing, 68th squadron at Ellsworth Air Force Base. I was a sergeant in the 44th Security Police Group, when the following incident occurred. The incident was never officially reported or documented—a mistake I have always regretted.

I was the flight security controller (FSC) at Launch Control Facility, (LCF) MIKE Flight, or "Mike-1", as it was known by military and civilians near Belle Fourche, South Dakota. I was in charge of classified, secret information regarding entry into an underground launch capsule, in which launch control officers prepared for nuclear war. Besides being responsible for certain equipment and classified information, I had the task of dispatching two-man security alert teams (SAT) to maintain the security of the ten launch sites (LS) over a tri-county area. It was commonly known that our presence was mostly "window dressing," but oddly enough, we helped keep the peace. To most of the local residents in this part of the northern Great Plains, we were a constant reminder of the perils of man's greatest folly—nuclear war.

At any given time, four launch control officers, a facility manager, six security police, and an indispensable cook were at the facility. The security police, today known as security forces, rotated their assignments every three days; twelve hours on, twelve hours off, with six days off-duty. This made the isolation and monotony of the work more bearable and far more attractive than other assignments in the one thousand-personnel-strong group.

On a late, beautifully clear, typically crisp night near the magnificent Black Hills, (a relatively short distance northwest of here and similar to the terrain in south-central Montana where General George Armstrong Custer met his fate), I received notification from the launch commander of a "situation" at one of the launch sites some miles away. Fortunately, my SAT was out on patrol and not far away from the site. The team notified me, and Central Security Control (CSC) at Ellsworth, who were monitoring all frequencies, as they were approaching the location. Then, I lost radio contact to an annoying hiss of static. This was of concern since I had noted some excitement in the voice of whoever was on the radio.

I do not clearly recall how long it was until I finally regained contact, but such loss of contact was not considered unusual in this expansive rural area. CSC never concerned themselves unless the FSC appeared not to be monitoring the circumstances at hand.

The first transmission I received was garbled and unusually excited, as I recall the team driver's voice. Airman Grossmann, a German immigrant, was talking mostly in English but inexplicably lapsed into German! The team leader, Airman First Class Baber, took control of the microphone, but I still couldn't understand what, if anything, was wrong. If they were under duress, such as being under fire, we would have immediately understood that. Clearly, something strange was happening, or had already happened!

At some point, I understood they were returning to the LCF, and I was relieved. I knew they would eventually explain what all the excitement was about. When my men returned (boys of nineteen and twenty—I was twenty two), they had quite a story to tell—if their faces didn't already say all we needed to know!

By now the relief FSC, my close friend and roommate, and his team were aware something had happened. I informed the launch commander and his relief, a captain, about the excitement going on. Both men were obviously in a state of agitation, and in Baber's case, he really just wanted to forget what had happen altogether.

Grossmann, now in control, explained clearly, succinctly, and as professionally as he could, what happened.

While performing the usual observation upon approach, then unlocking and entering the property of the site, they did the routine, mundane, systematic check, on foot, of the open air, fenced-in area (about an eighth of a mile square), when they were suddenly overcome by a high-intensity "fall of light." They were unable to determine the origin. Trained to defend themselves, they knew how to challenge virtually any threat that was presented to them, but they heard nothing and saw nothing except this unexplained, intense light over the site. They retreated to the LCF, due to the lack of communication and to wait for further orders.

We discussed the situation all too briefly. Essentially, the senior officer, a captain, likely concerned about his career, impressed upon us that this "can of worms" should not be opened, as it would then go to a higher authority. He suggested that we'd all have to endure and undergo "de-briefs"(interrogations) and possible therapeutic treatment for "mental stability." I mentioned that CSC may want a follow-up and the same officer quickly suggested that he would handle it. Everyone decided to forget about it. I never did. I seriously doubt they did either.

These incidents were not uncommon and occurred at many of the USAF military installations—over a long period of time—and mostly at sites where nukes were present.

I share this information now because such incidents are something that people in a so-called "free country" should know about. Besides, if an intelligent entity was interested in Earth's people, wouldn't they be concerned about our weapons capability?

The light was very intense and concentrated. It appeared very suddenly. It occurred outside and was blinding to the men. There was nothing to ever account for it.

Personally, I don't believe it originated from anything on this planet at that time. Neither do a number of other Air Force personnel who have had similar experiences.

—*Val Rosales, sergeant, retired*
United States Air Force Security Police

Recovery Under the Mackinac Bridge

In September 1989, a young woman was driving northbound on I-75, crossing the Mackinac Bridge from the Lower Peninsula to the Upper Peninsula of Michigan, in a late-model subcompact car. It was late at night, raining, and very windy.

She lost control of the vehicle and veered from the inside lane of the divided roadway to the outside lane. Somehow, the car jumped the guardrail and traveled over the side of the bridge structure. The car and driver fell 180 feet to the water below, where they quickly submerged and sank to the bottom of the Straits of Mackinac. Rescue boats searched the waters, but found no trace of the vehicle or driver.

At the time, I was assigned to the Michigan State Police Underwater Recovery Unit, and sent to meet with several other unit members in Mackinaw City on the south end of the bridge. The team arrived at Mackinaw City three days prior to the day of the recovery dive. We met with the state police from the Cheboygan Post, DNR marine officers, U.S. Coast Guard, bridge authorities, and local law enforcement.

The first objective was to brief everyone about the accident. A strong wind continued to blow for the next two days, so we had time to recreate the accident scene and plan for the recovery attempt. On the third day, the wind and waves had settled enough to start the recovery dive. My assigned partner and I were the first two divers to make the descent to the bottom, 156 feet below. We had an approximate location from United States Coast Guard sonar, where they had placed a 500-pound concrete block on the bottom as near to the vehicle as possible.

Divers used a line attached from the bridge railing where the car went over, to the concrete block on the bottom. My dive partner and I started down the ascent/descent line toward the bottom. The current was flowing from east to west through the Straits of Mackinac at about four knots that morning. We turned on our dive lights at about sixty feet and continued our descent.

The bottom came into view from about ten feet above, and we started our search for the vehicle, with me making a 360-degree sweep at the end of a twenty-five foot length of line. I found some debris from the inside of the car lying on the bottom, but not the car. Our plan was to make the sweep and return to the dive boat even if the car was not located. Our time on the bottom was limited at that depth, and we would soon have to start our slow return to the surface.

However, my dive partner tied another length of line that he had to the first and set off on his own. I stayed at the concrete block and started checking my dive computer. Much to my surprise, I was running low on air and my tissue gases were nearing maximum levels. I gave the emergency signal by jerking the search line three times to recall my dive partner. But, the line was slack. I decided that I couldn't leave my partner, because he might not be able to locate the line he left on the bottom and would likely have to make an emergency ascent to the surface. Due to the current, he would have been carried far from the dive boat and into the area where many civilian observer boats were riding around to watch the show.

I decided to swim to the end of the search lines to see if I could find him. Once there, I could see a dive light about thirty feet away. He had located the car, and had detached himself from the search line so he could reach it. I kept signaling him with my light, but it seemed like forever before he noticed and swam to me. I immediately started swimming back to the ascent line with my dive partner behind me.

As I made the turn upward at the concrete block, I drew my last breath from my tank. It was 115 feet to the first decompression station, where another diver was waiting with spare scuba tanks. I knew I couldn't make it that far and turned to my partner for his octopus regulator so we could buddy-breathe and make a safe ascent. I didn't know he had sacrificed his octopus regulator for an air hose to feed his dry suit (I was diving in a wet suit). The only option was to buddy-breathe using his one regulator. He took a breath and gave me the regulator. I was to take three breaths and give it back so he could take three breaths. The problem was that when I took three breaths I needed 300 to catch up. We buddy breathed twice and then I decided to take my chances and head to the surface as fast as I could. My dive partner tried to hold me back because of the danger of making a "blow and go" emergency ascent.

Even before I left my dive partner, my lungs were burning and in pain. I knew I was in trouble. But, in a moment, the pain went away. I was beginning to lose consciousness. I felt quite peaceful. I was still headed for the surface, exhaling the expanding air in my lungs. I was thinking that I had finally "bought the farm"—my expression for dying. I was sure I was going to die, and I accepted this fate.

I kept my hand on the line as I continued my nearly unconscious ascent. I don't know how deep I was when I noticed the safety diver above me. I stopped when I reached him, but didn't have the ability to put the regulator he was holding in my mouth. So, he put it in my mouth and purged the water out so I could breathe. Fortunately, I had enough consciousness left to do that part—breathe.

Just as suddenly, I realized I wasn't going to die after all. The safety diver was on wire communications with the dive boat. They had been worried about my partner and me because we were way beyond our time limit for the depth we were working in. I had to stay at the forty-foot level for what seemed to be a very long time to decompress. Finally, I was able to ascend to the thirty-foot stop, then twenty feet, ten feet and, at last, the surface.

I was extremely cold by that time and shivering uncontrollably. I was helped onto the dive boat and transferred to the Coast Guard buoy tender where I was put on oxygen. I was debriefed and taken below deck, where I laid on a bed for a long time.

As I began to relive the incident, anger at my dive partner emerged. I wondered if I should have left him and tended to my own safety. But, Michigan State Police Officers are not trained that way, and the highly specialized underwater recovery team members are even more dedicated to each other. In defense of my dive partner, the water depth surely affected our judgment—and he did find the car. However, I believed he had almost cost me my life.

The vehicle and driver were brought to the surface and transported back to Mackinaw City. The question is: What did I take away from this experience? I didn't see any bright lights or a glimpse of life beyond death—no angels or spiritual beings met with me. I was just lost in thoughts of my past and convinced I had bought the farm. It was a near-death experience. I thought about my family, but not in a how-are-they-going-to-get-along-with-me-gone way. They were part of my many thoughts. Maybe I wasn't far enough away from life at that point to see in that perspective. I wasn't panicked either, just peaceful. I'm not sure where I was, but I can say that I'm not ready to experience near death again.

What I gained was new appreciation for the transient nature of our life on earth. The experience changed my priorities in life. We are, too often, overwhelmed by the "white noise" in everyday existence and would do well to eliminate as much of it as possible. Life is not a condition to take for granted. Over-all, I look back at the recovery dive under the Mackinac Bridge as a useful learning experience. It certainly changed my diving methodology.

About three years later I retired from the state police and became a scuba instructor. I'm quite sure that my eighteen years experience on the Michigan State Police Underwater Recovery Unit, and especially that day in late September 1989, made me a better instructor. In my opinion, that's a pretty good deal in life.

—*Glenn Sanford, trooper, retired*
Michigan State Police

Re-Contact

September 12, 2010. Exact Time: Unknown

The first thing I remember is that I'm escorting a young woman into a craft of some type. I can't see what it looks like because we are so close and under it, but its big. We walk up a type of stairs into the craft. It was very dim and seemed to be lit up by different colored equipment lights. You could see fine, but it was darker. There was a large round seating area right in the middle of the craft where everyone was sitting, all facing out toward the sides of the craft.

There was a large area of space in the middle of the seating. There were approximately fifty people seated. Everyone except me seemed to be in a trance-like state with their eyes open. I could hear a voice as though it was coming to us telepathically, instructing us what to do. The craft began to spin, slowly at first. As soon as it began to pull at us—like being on a merry-go-round—the voice said, "Activate neutralizing."

At that time, in the center area where we all were sitting, we stopped moving. In the open center of the oval seating area a large ball of blue light was floating in the air. It was about three feet across and seemed to be spinning in the opposite direction of the craft. The outside part of the craft began moving very fast, but it had no effect on us.

Then this voice said, "Yes, people, this isn't a dream. You are in space." And with that, all of sudden we could see out every side of this craft as though it were made of glass, or maybe it was translucent. All I know is I could see planets, nebulas, and stars. I remember being so close to some rings of a planet that I thought we were going to hit them. It was just beautiful and amazing! I thought to myself, *How many times have I seen this? Why are we here?*

I got the sense or feeling this was like a "training flight" for the people on board, so they would know what to do and would know what to expect when the time came. I knew I was a trainer because I was the only one who had free will and had full control over myself. I already knew what to do and when to do it. I sensed knowing everything about the craft and what it was we were doing. I can't recall details of why, where, and how, but that didn't surprise me. I only remember what they let me remember. I can remember, when I looked at all the people sitting there, that I only recognized one person. It was a well-known newscaster. I know it sounds weird, but there he was, just sitting there like everyone else. I thought, *Why him?* Then I thought, *Why not him?*

The next thing I remember is being back at Earth and in a big city, like New York. We must have just dropped one or more people off and it was dark out. I could see the ground was wet, as though it had rained. We were at a large parking-lot-type of space. As we started to go back up, I was able to look out the back (maybe through a window, but I don't know) and I saw a guy at a little newsstand-type thing. He was looking up at us in the craft, and he had a look on his face of, *Oh my God ... they are real!* I thought to myself, *poor guy, no one will believe him if and when he says he saw a UFO!* Then we sped off so fast it was like a blur.

I remember dropping more people off, only this time I also remember giving them some kind of protein packs to eat or drink. It was something to help their bodies recover from what they had just gone though. I was told telepathically to make sure everyone had what they needed. The ground was brightly lit by some lighting from the craft, and I could feel electricity in the air. It kind of felt like the hairs on my arm wanted to stand up, and I seem to remember a slight smell of electricity—like the smoke you smell from a spark or hot wires. I seemed to be working very fast to get this all done. I was the only one that was doing this as far as I could see. When I felt like everything was done, I was suddenly at home again, sitting wide awake, and it was about 5:00 AM.

I immediately went to the kitchen table and started writing this all down. I had an adrenalin rush going, that's for sure. Even now, when I think about it, I get that feeling in the pit of my stomach. I had more aches and pains than normal. It was like I had done a lot of work—which I had.

When I look back at it all, I get the feeling that we were prepping these people so that when the time comes, people will be ready to go and know what to do when they go. They may not remember any of this prep work now, but it's locked away in their heads and ready to be used when the time is right.

My experience reminded me of all the police training we go through as officers, so that when and if a serious time comes, we can act without hesitation. We just do it. Is this why I have been taken since I was a child, so I could be trained my whole life to help and train people about something? I don't have answers, but I do have a gut feeling that this is not the only UFO craft around and these are not the only people being trained. I don't see this experience as a case of abduction, but rather as a case of rescue.

What will humans be saved from? I don't know. Is a serious situation getting closer and this is why I can remember more and more of my experiences? I feel like it is.

Lastly, this was not a dream. It was too real. Once again I am left with more questions than answers, but at least this time I have more of a "why" feeling than I had before, and that helps.

—Kent Milner, reserve officer, retired
Grandville Police Department

Rammed!

I was a three-year trooper when dispatched to assist in a car chase. Three subjects had stolen a brand new pickup truck from an elderly couple who had just moved north to a relatively quiet little town. It wasn't quiet on this day!

The subjects were driving the truck at extreme speeds up to 100 mph and headed southbound on US 131. They had already driven recklessly through two small towns and were headed south toward another. When I received the call for assistance, officers wanted to try and get the vehicle stopped before it traveled through another small town.

I arrived to a location on US 131, a two-lane highway, well ahead of the stolen vehicle. I did not have the mats to roll out on the highway, which punctures tires when run over and is the safest way to deflate tires and bring vehicles to a screaming halt, in my opinion.

Since my department didn't have this equipment at the time, I thought long and hard about what I could do. I decided to pull out onto the roadway, well ahead of the fleeing vehicle, and then force it to slow down by not allowing it to pass me.

Officers from three different departments were chasing the vehicle and I could hear their location on the radio. I was parked near the village of South Boardman, and I pulled onto the highway well ahead of the vehicle. Eventually, I saw the patrol car lights behind the vehicle through my rear view mirror. The vehicles were gradually gaining ground on me.

I kicked up the accelerator and reached a traveling speed of 90 mph. The truck was still gaining on me, with all the patrol cars behind it, but the truck did not appear to be slowing down. I raised my speed to 95 mph. Fortunately, there were no vehicles coming from the opposite direction and I had a long, clear distance ahead of me. I basically had the whole roadway to myself.

The truck got closer and closer, which means it was still going faster than me. I edged to the left, barely crossing the center line. I wasn't going to let this truck pass me. As it came right up to my rear bumper, I suddenly lost total control of my vehicle.

Thoughts, visuals, family members, friends, experiences, feelings, life successes, and regrets—going all the way back to childhood—raced through my mind in only three seconds. It was the most peaceful (believe it or not), timeless experience I ever had, because I really thought I was going to die. My car was traveling so fast that there was no way in hell that I could control it. So, I basically let go of the steering wheel to welcome God.

Those three seconds of thoughts and memories were in a nonphysical, but peaceful, space of existence. After regressing through all the memories in my life, I saw additional visions of war and peace, kings and queens, peasants and revolutions. I even heard bagpipes—and all in three seconds.

I still find that amazing. Someone told me that I experienced the Akashic Records.

I heard a voice in my head that said, "everything would be fine," as my car rolled and then crashed onto its top. When my car landed, it was lodged between two very large trees. As I am hanging upside down in my seat belt, I realize I'm okay, and I can hear people calling me on the radio.

Two troopers stopped from the chase and rushed to my aid. They kicked out my driver's side door window. As I'm trying to answer the radio, Trooper Bonnie Craig, a friend and more experienced trooper, blocked my hand from keying the mike. I thought I was of sound mind, but she understood differently. She didn't want me saying anything to anyone until I fully recovered and recuperated from the initial trauma. I remember the sergeant asking over and over on the radio if I had lost control of my vehicle.

I said to Trooper Craig, "But, I think I *did* lose control of the car. It was my fault! I just want to say I'm okay."

Trooper Craig immediately responded, "No, you were *rammed!* That truck *rammed* you!"

I chuckled, thinking she is so smart to say this. I instantly thought she was protecting me because she was a union representative. I felt grateful that she would protect someone as green as me.

To my amazement, however, I really *was* rammed and didn't know it! It was all caught on in-car cameras, from the vehicles chasing the truck. I couldn't believe it. I truly thought that it was all my fault.

The truck eventually lost control in a town further south and officers arrested three uninjured juveniles. As for the retired couple's truck—it was totaled.

I had no injuries except for scratches from the broken glass I swept off. Thank God I am only five foot two and a fairly small person. I thank God for keeping me alive that day.

After this accident, I realized what my sole purpose was in life, which was to try and help police officers somehow. I realized they were my family. A trooper of average size (or bigger), probably wouldn't have survived.

—*Ingrid P. Dean, detective sergeant, retired*
Michigan State Police, Traverse City, Michigan

Biographies of Contributing Officers

Charles Allen, inspector, is retired from the Michigan State Police. Insp. Allen served thirty-three years in a number of capacities, including trooper, teacher, and detective sergeant in the state police polygraph unit. Allen was promoted to post commander in West Branch, Michigan, and then to assistant district commander—inspector for the Third District in Michigan. Insp. Allen retired in 2010.

John G. Arthur is an active-duty trooper with the Michigan State Police.

Lawrence A. Bak is an active-duty sergeant with the Michigan State Police. Sgt. Bak currently has over forty-one years of service, having served the Flint, Detroit Freeway, Erie, and Alpena posts throughout his career.

Scott R. Bates is an active-duty trooper with the Michigan State Police. Tpr. Bates has served nineteen years, with the last seventeen years at the Houghton Lake Post. Married for twenty-one years to his wife, Denise, Tpr. Bates has three children (all boys), ages eighteen, sixteen, and twelve. Active in the community as a coach and mentor, Bates coaches high school baseball, little league baseball, junior high football, and junior high basketball. Scott loves to hunt, fish, and spend time with his family.

L.L. Bean, detective sergeant, is retired from the Michigan State Police. Det. Sgt. Bean has over twenty-one years of law enforcement experience, with twelve years as a police polygraph examiner.

William Behling, sergeant, is retired from the United States Air Force Security Police. Sgt. Behling is a career proprietary security manager, marksmanship instructor, and an occasional contributor of articles to *Tiger Flight*, the official journal of the Air Force Security Forces Association.

Albert A. Boyce, detective sergeant, is retired from the Michigan State Police. Det. Sgt. Boyce joined the state police in 1974 as a service trooper (cadet), later graduating from Trooper School. He served at Tekonsha, Northville, and posts in Lansing and Flint, Michigan, before being promoted to C.I.D. and Traffic Services Division. During this time he became a commissioned officer in the armed services and is, in fact, presently employed as an army contractor running the Military Funeral Honors Program for the Michigan Army National Guard.

Ray Bronicki, sergeant, is retired from the Michigan State Police. After serving in World War II in the 3rd Marine Division, Mr. Bronicki joined the Michigan State Police in 1948. He was stationed at the New Buffalo, Detroit, East Tawas,

Brighton, and Niles Posts, serving at such junctures as the major prison riot at Jackson Prison in 1953 and the Detroit Riots in 1967, when forty-five people were killed.

Thomas A. Brosman, III is an active-duty, senior telecommunications specialist for the Washington State Patrol. Brosman is also a writer and has contributed several stories to notable publications and magazines. A native of Washington State, Brosman has served with the Washington State Patrol for over thirty years.

Herman Brown is an active-duty trooper and has been with the Michigan State Police for sixteen years, Tpr. Brown presently works at the Monroe Post in Monroe, Michigan. Born and raised in Detroit, Tpr. Brown graduated from Adrian College and served three years in the United States Marine Corps at Camp Pendleton as a military police officer. Married to his wife, Jill Brown, also a state trooper, Tpr. Brown then attended the 108th MSP Recruit School, serving at both the Erie and Monroe posts. Tpr. Brown enjoys working out, has been a past bodybuilder, and delivers meals on wheels to the elderly. Tpr. Brown asserts his beliefs in spirits and guardian angels and believes they visit us every day.

Thomas M. Curtis, lieutenant, is retired from the Michigan State Police.

Mark A. David, Chief of Police for the Oscoda Township Police Department in Oscoda, Michigan.

Ingrid Dean, detective sergeant, retired from active duty with the Michigan State Police in April 2011. Ingrid Dean is the compiling editor of this book. She graduated from the 106th Michigan State Police Recruit School, was a trooper patrol officer for six years, and promoted to polygraph examiner for twelve years. Dean was a field detective at the Traverse City Post. She was a forensic artist and facial reconstructionist from 1991 until her retirement in 2011. She enjoys writing, teaching, flying, and diving.

Michael G. DeVita, patrolman, is retired from the Lima Police Department, Lima, Michigan. Ofcr. DeVita served as a police officer for twenty-fife years, and spent more than five years as a military police officer in the Army National Guard and Reserves. Ofcr. DeVita has a bachelor of science in criminal justice and is married with two grown sons. A practicing Roman Catholic, Ofcr. DeVita asserts that he has had many unexplained incidents since he was a teenager, but most significantly as a police officer.

Robert J. Dykstra is an active-duty detective lieutenant with the Michigan State Police Polygraph Unit. Det. Lt. Dykstra began his law enforcement career with the Sandusky Police Department in Sandusky, Michigan, in 1981, then he attended the Michigan State Police Recruit School in 1986. A graduate from Michigan State University, Dykstra has served as a trooper, detective sergeant, and detective lieutenant for over twenty-four years.

Falen, Harold, trooper, is retired from the Michigan State Police; served over twenty-five years with his department.

Sarah C. Foster is an active-duty detective trooper and forensic artist with the Michigan State Police. Tpr. Foster specializes in two-dimensional composite drawing, age progression, fugitive enhancement, and facial reconstruction.

Kenneth Charles Golat is director and an active-duty officer with the Manistique Public Safety Department. Golat graduated high school in 1972 and attended Ferris State College in Big Rapids, Michigan. Upon graduation, Golat began his law enforcement career at the Mackinac Island Police Department, worked for the Mackinac County Sheriff's Department, Norway Police Department, and Dickinson County Sheriff's Department as a juvenile and probation officer. He joined the Manistique Public Safety Department in 1978 and became Director in July 2005. He has thirty-seven years in law enforcement.

Mary M. Groeneveld recently retired from the Michigan State Police after over twenty-five years of service.

Charlie Gross, detective sergeant, retired from the Michigan State Police after serving twenty-seven years. He resides in Marquette, Michigan, and is married with two grown daughters and one granddaughter. A 1970 graduate of Northern Michigan University, he obtained his bachelor of arts in psychology and served in the United States Army military police. After the military, Gross attended the 83rd Michigan State Police Recruit School in 1972, then served at the Flint Post Training Division, and Criminal Investigation Division in East Lansing, Michigan. During his latter assignment, Gross worked on the Organized Crime Team, Surveillance Team, Major Case Team, and the UPSET Narcotics Team, holding positions as trooper, sergeant, and detective sergeant.

Todd M. Heller is an active-duty detective with the Grand Traverse County Sheriff Department in Michigan. Heller is a United States Army veteran and police officer with over fifteen years of experience. His assignments have included road patrol, school liaison officer, community police officer, undercover narcotics, and rescue diver. His most recent assignment is running the computer forensic laboratory and investigating computer-related crimes. Heller is a member of the Internet Crimes Against Children (ICAC) Task Force. He conducts forensic examinations of computers and other digital medias.

Donald Hinds, trooper, is retired from the Michigan State Police. Hinds joined the Michigan State Police in 1955, served at the Romeo, St. Ignace, and Iron River Posts, and then retired after thirty-five years of service. Hinds shares that Judge Roland Beeck in his story "The Apple Tree" is a witty, comical person, and liked by most!

Chip Horvarter is an active-duty police officer for the Bronson Police Department, Bronson, Michigan. Horvarter has been a police officer for over twenty years and was born in a police family, his father having served and retired after twenty-five years in the Michigan State Police. Ofcr. Horvarter presently works the night shift.

Craig W. Johnson is an active-duty trooper for the Michigan State Police in West Branch, Michigan.

Reuben R. Johnson, lieutenant, is retired from the Michigan State Police. Born to Finnish parents in the Upper Peninsula of Michigan, Johnson graduated from high school and briefly worked at a saw mill before joining the United States Navy. After discharge, he worked in a copper mine before joining the Michigan State Police in 1961. Upon graduation from recruit school, Ofcr. Johnson served at the Ypsilanti, Stephenson, Brighton, Blissfield, Detroit, and Northville posts, finally retiring in 1989 as a lieutenant in charge of the 7th District Traffic Services Unit in Traverse City, Michigan.

Rick Jones is an active-duty trooper with the Michigan State Police. Tpr. Jones is a seven-year veteran and works out of the Bridgeport Post, Saginaw, Michigan. Jones expresses great satisfaction working in his post area, including Saginaw City and County, stating there is always something going on.

Robert P. Landry, retired Louisiana state trooper. Landry served more than thirty-three years in law enforcement— twenty-five years with LSP and eight and a half years with two other law enforcement agencies. Landry has spent eight years working criminal interdiction upon Louisiana highways, with the last nine years served as a police polygraph examiner.

Duane H. LeRoy, chief of police, is retired from the Leslie Police Department in Leslie, Michigan. After graduating from high school, LeRoy worked at General Motors for six years, eventually graduating from Lansing Community College in 1976. LeRoy began his law enforcement career with the Leslie Police Department, and then joined the Ingham County Sheriff's Department, Delhi Division, in 1977. LeRoy served this department for twenty-two years, retiring in March 1999. He became Chief of Police for Leslie Police Department in October 2000, retiring again in 2006.

Robert Marble was an active-duty trooper with the Michigan State Police when he submitted his story "An Angel's Warning." Ironically, he passed away in an off-duty auto accident shortly after submitting his account. His daily presence is sorely missed by his family, fellow officers, and friends.

Jonathan Matteson is an active-duty United States Army security police. Presently serving in Alaska, Matteson is getting ready for deployment to Afghanistan.

A. Miller is an active-duty detective sergeant with the Michigan State Police.

Kent Milner, reserve officer, is retired from the Grandville Police Department in Grandville, Michigan.

Charles W. Newsome, sergeant, is retired from the Detroit Police Department. During his tenure with the Detroit Police Department, Newsome combated organized Latin gang activity both in the city and regionally. He was instrumental in developing actionable methods for understanding the historical, linguistic, cultural, and criminal enterprise interests and interrelationships of these gangs. Over his twenty-year career, Newsome made more than 2,000 felony arrests, was involved in scores of major police actions, and was injured in the line of duty on several occasions.

Larry D. Nichols is an active-duty chief of police for Scottville Police Department in Scottville, Michigan. After working as a supervisor in local manufacturing plants in Ludington and Scottville after high school, Chief Nichols joined the Scottville Police Department. Chief Nichols has served his department for over thirty-two years.

Daniel C. O'Riley, detective lieutenant, is retired from the Wexford Country Sheriff's Department in Cadillac, Michigan. O'Riley attended Holy Redeemer school throughout elementary, middle, and high school, and is a Vietnam veteran (served from 1968–1972). He joined the Wexford County Sheriff's Department in 1977, was promoted to detective in

1983, became detective sergeant in 1989, and was promoted to detective lieutenant in 1999. O'Riley retired in 2009 and received the FBI AA Award of Excellence for participation in solving the Hansel Andrews murder case.

John R. Patterson, retired military sergeant, is native to Richmond, Virginia. He started his law enforcement career in the US Army Military Police Corp, graduating from the Virginia Commonwealth University with a BS in administration of justice. After his military service, Patterson worked in corrections, probation/parole, and police polygraph.

Vernon R. Petersen, detective lieutenant, is retired from the Michigan State Police. Petersen served over thirty years as a trooper, detective sergeant, and detective lieutenant. The majority of Petersen's career was as a police polygraphist, at the Michigan State Police Marquette Crime Laboratory in Marquette, Michigan. Since retiring from law enforcement, Petersen continues his polygraph career as a private examiner throughout the State of Michigan and beyond.

William "Pete" Piazza, SM sergeant, retired from the United States Air Force (USAF) after serving as an air policeman/security policeman with the USAF from 1960 to 1988, which included three tours to Vietnam, and eleven assignments to bases all over the world, including Okinawa and the Philippines. A decorated air police officer, Piazza retired in 1988 and continued his law enforcement career for ten more years as a civilian officer with the Department of Veteran's Affairs.

Anthony V. Rosales, sergeant, retired from the US Air Force Security Police. Rosales was born in Los Angeles, California, and played high school and college football (quarterback in college), before joining the United States Air Force in 1970 and serving four years active-duty and six years reserve. Rosales served mostly at Andrews AFB and did a European tour of fourteen months to Turkey, Italy, Germany, and the United Kingdom. After the military, he worked as a security agent and police officer for Los Angeles County, California. Divorced with two grown children, Rosales loves motorcycling and shooting sports.

Glenn Sanford, trooper, is retired from the Michigan State Police Underwater Recovery Unit (URU). Sanford served twenty-six years as trooper on patrol, with eighteen years committed to the URU. Upon retirement, Sanford was certified as a scuba diver instructor and taught police and sport diving for several years.

Ted Schendel, sergeant, retired from the Ft. Lauderdale Police Department. Born in Dearborn, Michigan, Schendel attended Michigan State University and then went south for employment. He served twenty-four years with the Ft. Lauderdale Police Department and retired as a sergeant. He is married with two grown daughters, both seeking law enforcement careers.

Scott Schwander is an active-duty deputy with the Grand Traverse Sheriff's Department with over 20 years service. Prior to working for the county, Dpty. Schwander was a tribal conservation officer for his tribe. Scott enjoys playing the Native American and Anasazi flutes, bead working, boating, and family genealogy. He is presently assisting an author in documenting, on the Internet, the "Men of Company K, 1st Michigan Sharpshooters," an all-Indian battery of Civil War soldiers 1861–1865.

A. A. Seller is an active-duty detective sergeant with the Michigan State Police, who has over twenty-one years of service to the department.

Stephen C. Sokol is a newly retired officer from the Detroit Police Department, having served over twenty-four years as a patrol officer, police pilot, and bomb technician. Sokol shares that he has always had faith in God, but that the events which occurred in his story "An Angel's Shield," have now strengthened his beliefs and faith even more.

Steven R. Standfest, lieutenant, retired from the Beverly Hills Police Department in Beverly Hills, Michigan. He has a BA from Wayne State University and a MA from University of Detroit. He graduated from the 178th session of the FBI National Academy in Quantico, Virginia. After a career in law enforcement, Standfest is now an investigator conducting national security clearance background investigations. He enjoys hunting, Michigan fishing, and saltwater fishing in the Florida Keys.

Michael Thomas, patrolman, retired from the Flint City Police Department. Thomas worked as a patrol officer from 1968 to 1988 in a marked city police unit in Flint, Michigan.

Michael F. Thomas, retired, was a captain with the Michigan State Police.

Dawn Wagoner, an active-duty detective with the Grand Traverse County Sheriff's Department in Traverse City, Michigan, is currently assigned as a child abuse/sexual assault investigator. Det. Wagoner, a seventeen-year police veteran, worked as a patrol deputy for two years before being assigned to the Detective Bureau in 1996. Det. Wagoner has held a myriad of positions, including crime laboratory evidence technician, and police school liaison officer. Det. Wagoner is a 1993 graduate of Ferris State University.

Michael Wheat is an active-duty detective with the Charlevoix Sheriff's Department in Michigan. Wheat has served over twenty-five years in law enforcement and asserts his trust and faith in God.

Alan L. White is an active-duty patrol officer with the Clare Police Department in Clare, Michigan. Ofcr. White is a twenty-seven-year police veteran of law enforcement, having served in both Skagway, Alaska, and in Michigan. Ofcr. White is the author of four books, including *Alaska Behind Blue Eyes*, *Standing Ground*, *Promise Not to Tell*, and *In Sheep's Clothing*. He is also part-owner of a new bakery in Clare, Michigan, owned by fellow officers called "Cops and Donuts."

Vergil Lewis Williams, sergeant, retired from the Amarillo City Police Department. Williams asserts that his police career spanned only a six year period, but that it changed his life forever. He obtained a bachelor of science in economics, continued on to graduate school, and eventually obtained his PhD in 1972. Williams entered the teaching field in criminal justice, partly due to his police experience, and has felt privileged to develop college courses and contribute to the emerging scholarly field of criminal justice, academic research, and literature.

Duane Wright is an active-duty deputy with the Leelanau Sheriff's Department in Suttons Bay, Michigan.

What's Next?

Would you like to read more stories like this? ***Please spread the word!*** Ingrid Dean is seeking additional miracle police stories for a follow-up book from civilian and military police officers, 911 dispatchers, correctional officers, civilian support staff, police chaplains, police psychologists, spouses, and police family members. If you have seen or experienced anything exceptional, strange, or unexplainable in police work—anything that goes beyond the realm of normal expectations, to whatever degree—please share your experience with us. All contributors will receive a free, signed copy of the next book if your story is chosen for printing.

Most importantly, the purpose of compiling another book in this series is three-fold:

1. To share the extraordinary, spiritual, human side of the law enforcement community.

2. Collectively give readers a glimpse of what it's like to be in law enforcement and to read about the exceptional human experiences we have.

3. To help civilians see law enforcement from various perspectives, yet in a positive light—as men and women with varying belief systems who care deeply for the communities they serve.

Your police support would be greatly appreciated. Stories can be kept confidential and anonymous. The author is especially aware that stories may relate to sensitive issues and will work with you to ensure legal and privacy safeguards.

To obtain a copy of our submission guidelines, please contact:

Ingrid P. Dean, Llewellyn Publishing, LLC, or contact author directly at her website: www.spiritofthebadge.com.